Narcissist

This Book Contains 2 Manuscripts: Narcissist and Empath

Discover These Two Particular Personalities That Often Attract Each Other.

By Victor Murphy

Legal Disclaimer

The information contained in this book and its contents is not designed to replace any form of medical or professional advice; and is not meant to replace the need for independent medical, financial, legal, or other professional advice or services that may be required. The content and information in this book have been provided for educational and entertainment purposes only.

The content and information contained in this book have been compiled from sources deemed reliable, and they are accurate to the best of the Author's knowledge, information, and belief. However, the Author cannot guarantee its accuracy and validity and therefore cannot be held liable for any errors and/or omissions. Further, changes are periodically made to this book as needed. Where appropriate and/or necessary, you must consult a professional (including but not limited to your doctor, attorney, financial advisor, or other such professional) before using any of the suggested remedies, techniques, and/or information in this book.

Upon using this book's contents and information, you agree to hold harmless the Author from any damages, costs, and expenses, including any legal fees, potentially resulting from the application of any of the information in this book. This disclaimer applies to any loss, damages, or injury caused by the use and application of this book's contents, whether directly or indirectly, whether for breach of contract, tort, negligence, personal injury, criminal intent, or under any other circumstance.

You agree to accept all risks of using the information presented in this book.

You agree that by continuing to read this book, where appropriate and/or necessary, you shall consult a professional (including but not limited to your doctor, attorney, financial advisor, or other such professional) before using any of the suggested remedies, techniques, or information in this book.

Narcissist

A Complete Guide to Dealing with a Range of Narcissistic Personalities

By Victor Murphy

Table of Contents

Introduction

We hear so many buzz words, seemingly on a daily basis, and one you will no doubt have heard thrown around quite commonly is 'narcissist', or 'narcissism'. These are of course one and the same thing.

This book is going to talk about this very subject and highlight the fact that whilst you might feel like you meet narcissists every single day of your life, a genuine narcissist is actually quite rare. What you're probably encountering is a person who has a generally inflated sense of self-importance, but one trait alone doesn't diagnose someone with a narcissistic tendency!

The thing is, most people have a slight narcissist tendency at some point in their lives. Sometimes we can be over-confident, sometimes we can put others down needlessly, and sometimes we can seek out validation for no reason. None of this means that we are a narcissist, unless there are several traits together, and it happens on a very regular basis.

You see, a true narcissist is actually a person who needs help, but the problem is that most of them will never admit they need it, and so therefore never really receive it. It's a sad fact, but one which is all too common. Narcissists, real ones, are actually rare, with the Diagnostic and Statistical Manual of Mental Disorders stating that between 0.5% - 1% of the US population has true narcissism, e.g. they have been diagnosed with Narcissistic Personality Disorder (more on that shortly). Within that, between half to three quarters are men. Of course, women can be equally as narcissistic, but it seems that more men display these traits on a regular basis.

Dealing with a narcissist, especially if you find yourself growing close to one, can be a very difficult situation to be in. You probably won't realize that they are actually narcissistic until you do grow close, because these types of people are masters of disguise. They will appear charming, aloof, and extremely attentive until they have you hooked. From then on, the traits appear, and emotional manipulation takes hold.

No, a narcissist isn't an evil person. A narcissist is someone who suffers from a genuine personality disorder. Despite that, it doesn't make being around one any easier.

This book is going to give you all the information you need on narcissism, and it's also going to help you understand how to deal with one in your life. If you are in a relationship with a narcissist, it may be time to think of yourself and actually get out, if you find that you can't help them, or they don't want to accept help.

It's sad but true that many narcissists are actually very lonely individuals, lacking in self-confidence and not really understanding why people react to them the way they do.
So, whether you have a narcissist in your life, you think you yourself might have narcissistic tendencies, or you're simply interested in learning more, this book will give you all the information you need.

Chapter 1
Definition of Narcissist

In general, the simple definition of a narcissist is:

"Someone who has an excessive interest or admiration of themselves"

Of course, nothing in this world is ever that simple, because the world of narcissism is actually a deep and complicated well of personality traits and problems. The problem with that definition is that there are many people on the planet who are self-absorbed and a little 'too into themselves', but they're not necessarily narcissistic; they're just vain.

It is for this very reason that the term 'narcissist' is thrown around and attached to people who don't actually fall under the remit. In one way, this is a disservice to that person, because as you'll see as we go on to explore what narcissism really is, nobody wants to be labelled with this term if they truly aren't! On the other hand, it's a disservice to those who do suffer from Narcissistic Personality Disorder (NPD), because it's no joke, and it's not a choice either.

You see, as we go through this book, you're likely to start developing a deep-seated dislike for narcissistic people, but before you get to that point, I want you to think a little deeper. A person suffering from depression isn't blamed for their condition. A person with anxiety isn't laughed at for worrying too much. A person with an eating disorder isn't avoided and belittled. NPD is a real thing, a personality disorder, which therefore falls under the mental health umbrella. Any such condition doesn't deserve belittling, it doesn't deserve name calling or avoidance. If anything, we should be trying to help these people, but the problem? Most narcissists don't realize there is anything wrong with them, and they certainly won't accept your help willingly.

It's a doubled edged sword which has very few positive outcomes for most people.

This chapter is going to give you the basic points of what it means to be a narcissist. We're going to talk about the history of narcissism, the types of narcissists you'll encounter in your life, and the traits which embody a true narcissist. Remember, if you read one or two traits and recognize them in yourself or your partner, don't automatically jump to conclusions that you have NPD. Real narcissists embody several, if not all, of the common traits.

What is a Narcissist?

A true narcissist is someone who suffers from Narcissistic Personality Disorder (NPD) and is a person who has an extreme interest in themselves, an inflated sense of self-importance, and someone who struggles to maintain relationships and friendships with other people. It's likely that a narcissistic will not have long-lasting friendships in their life, e.g. they won't have someone in their life who they've been friends with since childhood, whereas many other people will have at least one.

The reason for this is that narcissists push people away with their behavior, although they don't actually mean to do it. You see, narcissists aren't trying to hurt people intentionally, they simply do it through their actions, and don't see anything wrong with what they are doing. A narcissist is never wrong in a narcissist's eyes. A narcissist's opinion is not an opinion, it is fact - that is how they see it.

We're going to talk about the traits of a narcissist shortly, which will bring more understanding in terms of what a narcissist actually is. We're also going to talk about NPD in far greater detail too.

For now, you need to understand that NPD is a very real condition and one which falls under the personality disorder umbrella. Just like someone with imposter syndrome, borderline personality disorder, or bipolar disorder, NPD isn't something you can snap your fingers and 'get out of', it is an ingrained part of who a person is. It can be mild, moderate, or it can be severe. It can be there all the time, or it can be flared up by experiences and situations.

The hope is that this book achieves the following two things, at the very least:

- Helping someone who is affected by a narcissistic relationship
- Helping to bring awareness to the fact that narcissism is a real thing

Narcissism in History

It might feel like narcissism has only become a 'thing' recently, but it's actually not the case. What is true is that narcissism seems to be a common buzz word at the moment, but the very idea of narcissism actually started way back in Greek mythology. In this form, Narcissus was a man who fell so deeply in love with the image of himself in the water that he simply couldn't stop admiring the reflection. He eventually died at the spot through lack of nutrition. From that point, narcissism has been considered negative.

Of course, in order for the idea of narcissism to have made it all the way to this day and age, there needs to have been studies and research continuing. The first such known study was in 1911, by Otto Rank. Freud also published a study on narcissism in 1914, before the groundwork for recognizing NPD began in 1967, through a study conducted by Otton Kernberg and Heinz Kohut. It wasn't until 1980 that NPD was officially recognized as a personality disorder, along with diagnosis criteria laid out.

Over the last decade or so, the word 'narcissist' has become common in society, but as we have already explored, it has been tagged to people who don't necessarily deserve it. True narcissism is very rare, and whilst people may occasionally exhibit narcissistic traits, perhaps even for prolonged periods of time, in order to be diagnosed with NPD itself, the story has to be a little deeper.

Types of Narcissist You Might Encounter

A narcissist is an individual kind of deal, just like every person is unique. There are several specific types of narcissist to know about. There are three main types to cover.

- **The Classic Narcissist** - You'll hear this type of narcissist also called the high functioning narcissist, the exhibitionist, or the grandiose narcissist. This is the classic category type that most fall into.

- **The Vulnerable Narcissist** - You will hear this type also referred to as compensatory narcissists, closest narcissists, or fragile narcissists. This type of narcissist will also feel that they are over and above everyone else, but they do not like being the center of attention, which pulls them apart from our first classic type. Instead of being in the spotlight, they attach themselves to other people who are of high importance, or who they perceive to be 'special'.

- **The Toxic Narcissist** - You will hear this type of narcissist called the malignant narcissist also, and this is the type that you need to be avoiding at all costs. This type of narcissist exploits other people for their own gains, and they are extremely manipulative. They seek out those who they assume to be vulnerable, e.g. empathic people, shy people, and they manipulate for what they can gain. This type of person craves control and in some extreme cases, may actually enjoy seeing someone else in distress or suffering.

Of course, every person you come across is unique and that means that a narcissist isn't likely to fall specifically under one type; they may exhibit traits of either type, but they will have one dominant category.

Traits of a Narcissist

Now we know what a narcissist is, and we know that there is a specific condition related to it, let's cover the main traits of a narcissist. Remember, there are three main types we have covered, and certain types will have specific traits, e.g. a toxic narcissist will be extremely manipulative emotionally, whereas a classic narcissist is more likely to be concerned with inflated ego, or thoughts of self-importance.

In general, however, the following traits are connected to those with NPD:

- An overwhelming need for attention
- Can often appear very charming at first
- Extreme jealousy
- Expecting special treatment and quickly becoming angry or aggrieved when it doesn't arrive
- An inflated sense of self-importance
- Often inflating the importance of talents or achievements
- Overinflating their abilities, often in romance and sex
- Very sensitive and easily hurt - doesn't handle rejection well and often responds with anger, shame, or extreme humiliation
- Has a hard time maintaining relationships which are healthy, either friendships or relationships

- Indulges in regular fantasies about their success, appearance, or power, etc.
- Has no problem taking advantage of another person in order to achieve something, and will not feel guilty about it
- Lacking in empathy, often disregarding the feelings of other people, even those close to them
- Considering that only 'special people' can understand them and how unique they are
- Often looking for positive reinforcement from other people or praise
- The idea that their opinion is right, and everyone else's is wrong
- The idea that everything they do is right, and they are never wrong about anything
- Assuming that everyone will agree with them or do what they want
- Only ever wanting the best of everything
- Selfish and arrogant

As you can see, there isn't a whole lot of positive there, and for someone who is in a relationship with a narcissist, they are likely to find the entire experience quite tough.

Is a Narcissist Actually a Bad Person?

When you read about narcissism and you read the list of traits, it's very easy to simply jump to the conclusion that a narcissist is actually a very bad person who should be avoided at all costs. The thing is, it's never that simple. Remember, NPD is a very real thing and is a personality disorder which falls under the mental health remit. You don't automatically judge someone who is suffering from depression for being detached, and you appreciate it to be part of their condition. The same kind of compassion should be placed towards NPD to some degree, however it is very difficult to do that when a person is treating you badly.

Some types of narcissists are easier to deal with than others, but if you are in the company of a toxic narcissist, you will find it extremely difficult to disagree with the idea that he or she is just a bad person.

Perhaps the best way to answer this question is to separate narcissists, or those who exhibit signs of NPD into two camps - those who are trying to do good but end up being pulled back by their condition, and those who simply don't care about anyone else.

Every single person is unique and complex, and that means that you can't simply put an umbrella 'bad person' tag on everyone who has some degree of NPD; and remember, not every person with NPD has a full-blown version, some have a tinge of it, whilst others may experience it sometimes and not at others. Again, people are complex!

Chapter 2
Narcissist Personality Disorder and Treatment Options

We've talked about NPD a lot in passing, but we've not really delved into what it is and what causes it. This chapter is going to do exactly that.

We know that NPD is a personality disorder, and these types of conditions fall under the very large mental health umbrella. Most people consider depression, anxiety, stress, and schizophrenia as the only types of mental health condition, but the list is far longer than that. For instance, bipolar disorder, borderline personality disorder, eating disorders, etc.; these are all mental health conditions in their own right.

Personality disorders are a sub-category of mental health issues, and people with these types of disorders have unhealthy thoughts and thinking patterns, and they also have behavioral issues too. These types of thinking patterns are often very rigid, and it can take a large amount of therapy to challenge and change these patterns over time. Most people with personality disorders also have problems relating to and perceiving people and situations.

What Causes NPD?

Nobody really knows. It's not an easy question to ask what causes any type of mental health issue, even depression. Some people are more prone than others, and in the case of NPD, some people have it and others don't; some people have just a little and other people have a full-blown case. It's a mystery in some ways, but many studies suggest that the following issues may be risk factors for developing NPD in later life:

- Hereditary issues, e.g. genes, particularly those which have an impact on the connection between behavior and the brain, e.g. oversensitivity
- Negative experiences in early childhood, e.g. abuse or poor parenting techniques
- Psychological issues
- A large amount of criticism experienced
- Previous trauma
- Having unrealistic expectations

Narcissists are not born, they are made. Whilst genes play a part, it is thought that experiences have a greater influence on the development of NPD at any age. Of course, it doesn't happen overnight, but NPD can occur at any age. For the most part, however, it begins in childhood, due to negative experiences and as a result of poor parenting practices, such as being insensitive as a parent, or from over-pampering and over-praising.

The Diagnostic Criteria for NPD

Diagnosis of NPD can be difficult, and because most people with this condition don't really seek out help for it (most don't think there is anything wrong with them), then many practitioners don't really have a huge amount of experience in offering a diagnosis. What is more likely to happen is that a general practitioner (regular doctor) will refer someone with this type of problem to a mental health practitioner. From there, in order to be diagnosed with NPD, a person will need to **meet five (or more) of the following criteria**:

- An exaggerated sense of self-self-importance
- A believe that they are special and should only be associated with high-status individuals
- A need for excessive compliments and admiration
- An exaggerated sense of entitlement
- Takes advantage of, or exploits, other people
- A lack of empathy
- A believe that others are jealous of them, and also struggles with jealousy themselves
- Arrogance on a regular basis

The Actions and Thoughts of a Narcissist

Getting into the mind of a narcissist can be a difficult thing. Every person thinks and acts differently, and every person is unique in how they approach situations and react to them. A narcissist, on the other hand, has some specific behavioral patterns, which makes them stand out. Whilst there will be anomalies here and there because everyone is different, there are two main examples to look at.

Using Either Overt or Covert Methods

In order for a narcissist to manipulate a person or situation, so that their needs are met above everyone else's, they will use methods which are described either covert or overt. Overt methods are quite obvious, whereas covert methods are quite secret and go under the radar. The covert methods are often the most destructive to other people, and this is why many people who are in relationships with narcissists often struggle to leave; they start to question 'is it me or them'. A classic method here is called gaslighting, and we'll cover that in far more detail a little later on.

Generally speaking, a classic narcissist is always going to use overt methods, and a vulnerable type of narcissist will use covert methods. The problem is that toxic or malignant narcissists will probably use a clever mixture of both.

A Somatic or Cerebral Approach

This is about how a narcissist appreciates things, and themselves. A narcissist using somatic methods will be completely taken by the way they look, their body, and their general appearance. They will be extremely vain. A cerebral method, however, is using the brain, and appearing to be overly intelligent; this type of narcissist will go to great lengths to convince you that their opinion is indeed the only one we'll be taking any notice of.

It's important to try and identify the type of narcissist you're dealing with, and whilst that can sometimes be difficult to pinpoint exactly, you will certainly be able to identify the most dangerous type. A toxic or malignant narcissist will have no issue in hurting others and will show no remorse. This type of narcissist is damaging to everyone around them, and it's likely that a person who escapes a relationship with this type of narcissist will need emotional support, and possibly therapy, afterwards.

Of course, you might read this and wonder how a person can't see that there is something wrong with the way they are acting and thinking, but that is exactly what NPD does. Remember, NPD is a personality disorder, which creates a disordered way of thinking. A narcissist will 100% genuinely think that you are in the wrong, and that you should be seeing their uniqueness, that you shouldn't be arguing with them because they're right. They won't look at themselves and consider that maybe they're wrong, or maybe they could have dealt with the situation better; a true narcissist doesn't see an issue in the way they think or the way they act. In the case of a toxic or malignant narcissist, this type of person certainly sees no problem in hurting another person for their own gains either.

Why Most Narcissist Never Receive Treatment

The last paragraph should answer the question of why most narcissists don't seek out treatment. Most narcissists don't realize there is a problem, and if someone tells them they need help because they're showing narcissistic tendencies, they're likely to laugh and turn it around on the other person.

Of course, this isn't the case for everyone, and for a person who may have a mild case of narcissism, there might be a light bulb moment when they think 'hey, I wonder if that applies to me', when reading an article or after someone has pointed out that they're acting in a narcissistic way. This is a rarity, however, and it's extremely unlikely that a classic or vulnerable narcissist of the truest type will seek out help.

Will a toxic or malignant narcissist ever get help? In some cases, this does happen, but usually only after a rather self-destructive moment, or when they have hurt someone else extremely badly. If an extreme moment pushes them to a certain point, it may be that medical help is recommended, and possibly accepted. Despite that, it's still unlikely, and that in itself is a very sad fact.

Can Treatment be Successful?

There are many different types of treatment for NPD, but most of it centers around behavioral changes and challenging thought patterns. In some cases, extreme cases, hospitalization may be recommended, especially for extremely toxic narcissists who have driven themselves to a very self-destructive moment.

The problem is that most treatment tends to center around solving the incident, rather than solving the actual condition.

So, can treatment be successful? It can, when help is sought, but it takes a huge effort and commitment on the part of the narcissistic party. Treatment also isn't easy, and the same goes for any type of condition which requires cognitive behavioral therapy and challenging mindsets and thoughts. This isn't a treatment method which will be successful overnight and will require a long-term approach, with probably maintenance treatment beyond that.

Other Personality Disorders Related to Narcissism

Most personality disorders and some mental health issues are linked together in certain ways. For instance, a person who suffers from depression may also suffer from anxiety, because there is a close link. A person with stress may suffer from anxiety, for the same reason. A person with bipolar disorder may also have links with narcissism, and a person with a borderline personality disorder may also have NPD too.

Despite that, there are three main types of personality disorder which also link closely with NPD in particular:

- Antisocial personality disorder
- Borderline personality disorder
- Histrionic personality disorder

An experienced healthcare professional will be able to assess whether the specific type of personality disorder at large, however again, convincing someone to seek out help can be difficult, especially someone with NPD.

24

Chapter 3
Common Narcissistic Situations You May Encounter

Up to this point, we've talked about what narcissism is and we've described it, but in order to really show you how it affects people in real terms, we need to give a few examples and scenarios.

This chapter is going to talk about possible situations in friendship, family life, relationships, and working environments, where narcissism may play a part. Remember, these are only examples, but they highlight how narcissism is usually played exhibited in real life. We'll highlight the narcissist's point of view, and how it makes the other person/people feel too, to give a complete picture of the problem.

In these scenarios, you might feel that we're focusing on men, but it doesn't actually matter which gender the narcissist or other party is, it's more about the actual scenario and actions/thought processes. Despite that, there are a higher percentage of male narcissists on the planet than female.

Friendship Situations

Scenario 1

Two men are friends, one of which is a narcissist (undiagnosed). They haven't known each other for too long and simply met through acquaintances at work. They are sat talking over a drink one evening, discussing politics. The narcissist gives his view of the situation, speaking over everything which the other person says, and laughing whenever the other friend tries to argue a point. In the end, the narcissist simply labels his friend stupid for not understanding his view, and 'how it really is'.

- **The narcissist's view** - The narcissist cannot understand why his friend wouldn't see his point of view as valid and starts to wonder why he is even friends with this man if he can't grasp basic intelligence.
- **The friend's view** - The friend feels hurt and annoyed that his so-called friend called him stupid and wouldn't even listen to his view. He now considers his friend extremely arrogant and starts to wonder whether he should continue spending time with him.

Scenario 2

Two women are friends, however, one friend (non-narcissist) always feels belittled by the other one. This particular day they decide to go shopping together because there is a big party coming up and they both need new outfits. The narcissistic friend chooses an outfit and walks around the dressing room in a sense of self-importance, lapping up compliments from everyone. The other friend tries a dress on, but the narcissistic friend belittles her with a comment about how it doesn't suit her and turns the conversation around to how great her dress looks.

- **The narcissist's view** - The narcissist thinks she looks fantastic in her dress and wants everyone to tell her so. She also needs everyone to tell her so, to give her the confidence to buy it.

- **The friend's view** - The friend is upset that she didn't pay any attention to what she was wearing and threw an offhand comment about it not suiting her. She felt disappointed and hurt, but then, it's always that way.

Family Situations

Scenario 1

A brother and sister are visiting their parents for Sunday lunch. The brother is narcissistic. Instead of allowing his sister to tell their parents what she has been doing that week, the brother talks endlessly about his week and how he impressed his manager. Every time his sister tries to interject, he simply dismisses her talk and continues his own tale.

- **The narcissist's view** - His sister's week was average and not worth talking about, he was full of success and he wants to share it with his family.

- **The sister's view** - Yet again her brother isn't letting her talk about her achievements, even though she was really proud of the presentation she gave at work that Wednesday. She simply keeps quiet and lets him talk, as always.

Scenario 2

Two brothers are helping their parents move to a new house and they come across several boxes of old things from their childhood. One brother's box is in the way of the other brother's box (the narcissistic brother's box is at the back). Rather than simply moving it out of the way, the narcissistic brother kicks it to one side, thus landing in a large puddle of garage oil. He pushes it with such force that it falls over and everything lands in the oil. The other brother's things are therefore almost ruined, but the narcissistic brother doesn't even bat an eyelid - he was head boy at school, so his childhood photos are more important.

- **The narcissist's view** - He wanted to get to his box of things to relieve his wonderful childhood achievements. He knows that his other brother didn't come anywhere near to his achievements, so what's the point in looking in his box?

- **The brother's view** - He is angry that his things are now ruined, and that his brother considers his childhood memories and belongings to be more important than anyone else's. This then results in a fight which he will never win, because his brother isn't even listening.

Relationship Situations

Scenario 1

A man and a woman are in a relationship which is almost reaching the year-long mark. The woman is going out for the evening with her friends, to celebrate a birthday. She comes downstairs wearing a dress, feeling really happy with the way she looks. Her boyfriend (narcissist) laughs at her and tells her the dress makes her look 'dumpy' because she's so short. Her good mood disappears, and she decides not to go out as a result. The boyfriend then suggests they spend the night in together because he wants her 'all to himself'.

- **The narcissist's view** - He didn't want her to go out because there were going to be too many men in the room and people would look at her in a short dress. He's instead happy that they're going to watch a film together and order a takeaway.

- **The girlfriend's view** - She thought she looked great and expected her boyfriend to compliment her but as soon as he told her she didn't look good, she lost all interest and confidence. She stayed in because if she had gone out anyway, she knew he would have been in a bad mood when she returned home. What's the point anyway?

Scenario 2

A woman is on her phone in the living room, idly scrolling through Facebook and checking her messages. She is smiling at something she has just seen on her Timeline. She puts down her phone and goes to the toilet. Her boyfriend (narcissist) wants to know why she was smiling, assuming that she was messaging another man. He takes her phone and because he knows the passcode, he looks at her messages. He sees a message from someone called 'David'. He immediately flies into a jealous rage, demanding to know who David is. David turns out to be her cousin, asking how her mum is.

- **The narcissist's view** - She has been smiling at her phone and engrossed in it for the last half an hour, she must be doing something. Who is David? How could she cheat on me? He basically flies into a jealous rage, not taking the time to actually read the message.

- **The girlfriend's view** - Completely offended that he thinks she would cheat in him, especially as she was doing nothing wrong. He's always like this, always jealous over petty things. He won't say he's sorry and she knows it.

At Work Situations

Scenario 1

A narcissistic woman works in an office and is always trying to make friends with management. She doesn't bother to speak to her colleagues or spend time with them, she would much rather try and become closer to those who she seems to be 'worth her time'.

- **The narcissist's view** - Management understand her and how special she is, they understand her potential and she is going to achieve. Why should she bother spending time with those below her?

- **Her colleagues' view** - She's always trying to get on side with management, it makes us all feel sick. Why does she think she is so special?

Scenario 2

In a brainstorming session, one employee (male narcissist) suggests something which he believes to be the answer to the entire problem at hand. His colleagues simply note it down but don't give it much praise. The narcissist cannot believe that his colleagues can't see how fantastic his suggestion is. Instead of wasting time, he goes to his manager and explains his idea instead, not bothering to wait for the final outcome.

- **The narcissist's view** - The idea he just came up with is perfect, why can't these people be able to see that? He believes that his manager understands him better anyway, so he goes to talk to him and puts his idea forward.

- **The manager's view** - Although the manager appreciates employees' ideas, and he has an open-door policy for suggestions, the employee displayed a certain air of forced authority which didn't come over as very welcome to the manager. The manager can't understand why the employee didn't simply allow the idea to be noted down with everyone else's and discussed as one.

As you can see, these scenarios point out some of the common narcissistic traits that you'll see in everyday life. Whilst you'll see these types of examples from general people who might be acting in a slightly narcissistic way, it doesn't mean that they are a narcissist! As we've mentioned several times, someone who wants praise doesn't necessarily fit the bill for narcissist diagnosis; they might simply be lacking in confidence at that time and want a little extra support. A person who acts in a jealous way over his girlfriend one or two times isn't necessarily a narcissist, they might be feeling insecure in the relationship due to a problem.

It's important to see the bigger picture, rather than simply jumping to conclusions and assuming that you are dealing with a narcissist. What these examples do however is show you just how annoying and upsetting a narcissist can be when they do things which belittle or upset someone close to them.

Working with a narcissist isn't easy, that's for sure. You'll find that narcissists try and enamor themselves with managers and those in authority because their inflated sense of importance leads them to believe that they are simply paying their dues in the office/another workspace, and that they are soon going to be promoted to a higher level anyway. In addition, a narcissist will push their ideas over everyone else's, and probably stamp over anyone who gets in their way.

What we haven't mentioned is the possible scenarios of a very damaging type of narcissist - the toxic or malignant narcissist. These types of scenarios can be very damaging and very dark indeed. For instance, emotional abuse at the hands of a narcissist of this type can be extremely mentally damaging to a person. This can be a family member, friend, relationship partner, or manager. Being constantly belittled, beaten down emotionally, and made to feel like everything is your fault can push someone towards a mental breakdown.

As we've mentioned before, and we'll certainly mention again in our next chapter, being in a relationship with a toxic or malignant narcissist is a form of abuse. The person won't notice it at the time, they'll be convinced it's them doing something wrong, purely because the narcissist is telling them that (gaslighting).

It doesn't have to be a relationship, it can be a parent who is narcissistic to this degree towards their child. In this case, the child is very likely to grow up with severe trauma and have issues of their own throughout their adult life. This in itself is likely to cause the toxic narcissism trait to continue onwards and taint that child's life in the years to come.

Whilst narcissism can simply be annoying, it can also be extremely dark and damaging too.

Chapter 4
How to Survive a Narcissistic Relationship

Most people are open to the idea of meeting a partner and having a healthy, loving relationship. This is what most people aim towards, and even if it isn't your final aim in life, most of us enjoy the process. What we don't enjoy is meeting someone who is unable to have that kind of healthy relationship.

A narcissist finds it extremely difficult to maintain healthy, loving relationships. The reason isn't clear, and it can vary from person to person; it could be because they experienced a lack of affection when they were a child, it could be because they've been hurt before and as a result they are using defense tactics, or it could be because they exhibit very jealous traits which make it borderline impossible for another person to live with. Of course, there is also the rest of the narcissistic spectrum of traits to take into account, which makes it very difficult for someone to maintain a relationship in a healthy way, with someone who has NPD.

When we meet someone we like, we know that there is a chance we are going to get our heart broken, and whilst we hope that it won't happen, we know that it is a possibility. We try not to let this bother us and simply move on with the fun side of a relationship. The problem is, a narcissist doesn't have the right amount of empathy or trust for a relationship to be anything but chaotic and emotionally damaging for the other person. As a result, many narcissists end up alone in the long-run. Most partners eventually leave, because they simply can't take it anymore; it can be a mild reason, or it can be something more severe, such as emotional abuse and gaslighting techniques.

We've mentioned gaslighting a few times already, but if you're not sure what it is, we're going to cover that in more detail in this very chapter. Whilst gaslighting isn't only found in narcissist relationships, it is quite common in this type of union.

We also know that there are more male narcissists on the planet than women. In that case, it's more likely that the male partner will be narcissistic towards the female, but that shouldn't lead you to believe that it is never the other way around. Just as there are many relationships which involve emotional abuse from the female partner to the male, there are also female narcissistic relationships too, either same-sex or female to male. People are people at the end of the day, and a narcissist is a narcissist whether male or female.

What most people don't understand about relationships with narcissists is how it actually got to the point of being a relationship in the first place. Surely if someone is being treated badly from the start they would leave before emotions got involved? Let's explore that in more detail.

A Wolf in Sheep's Clothing

One way to describe a narcissist in a relationship is like a wolf in Little Red Riding Hood. The wolf was clever and dressed up as someone Red could trust, i.e. her grandmother. By doing that, he appeared to be something he wasn't. Many narcissists do this without even realizing it.

When you first meet a narcissistic in a potentially date-like or attraction situation, they will be on their best behavior. He or she will be as charming as can be. Nobody really knows why this is the case, but it is thought to be down to their deep-seated desire to be liked and approved of. When they see someone they like, their desire is to potentially 'own' that person. Not in the actual ownership sense, but in a 'look what I managed to attract' kind of way. It sounds terrible, but that is how the mind of a narcissist operates at the first signs of attraction.

When a man or woman meets someone, who is on their best behavior, charming the socks off them and complimenting them on everything they say and do, it's hard not to become enamored. It's also worth pointing out that certain types of narcissists, especially the toxic ones, tend to focus on those who are a little emotionally weak or vulnerable. This makes the first stages of attraction far easier to navigate; someone who is quite vulnerable is probably going to overlook a few red flags, compared to someone who is strong and has a high level of self-worth. In that case, a person is far more likely to walk away at the first sign of an issue.

Once that first flush of attraction begins, the narcissist will keep up the wolf in sheep's clothing act until their partner is totally hooked. By that point, all bets are off. By that point, the true colors start to show.

This is why so many men and women end up in relationships with narcissistic partners. They have been tricked by an illusion.

Of course, not every narcissist is like this; we are painting a picture of the very worst type of narcissist here. Having said that, it is a common way for people to become close to those who do have narcissistic traits. In addition, it could be that an empathic person, or someone who has a natural tendency to want to help others, see the damaged side of a narcissistic and wants to make them 'better'.
You cannot make a narcissistic better. You cannot change them and heal them, but it doesn't stop some people from trying. One of the most toxic combinations in romance is a narcissist and an empath, and it is for this very reason. We're going to cover that particular subject in a little more detail shortly.

Signs You Are in a Relationship with a Narcissist

If you're in a relationship currently and you're looking at your partner and thinking 'you might be a narcissist', or you simply want to know what to look out for in the future, let's check out some of the most common signs that you are indeed in a relationship with a narcissist.

- **He or She Hijacks Every Conversation** - If you're out on a date, or you're simply chilling at home, and he or she always turn every conversation around to themselves, you're looking at narcissism territory. Narcissists love to hear their own voice and they love to talk about themselves and what they've done. If you manage to get a word into the conversation, then it's likely that whatever you say will be ignored or thrown to one side. When you start talking, they will probably interrupt you and turn everything back to themselves.

- **Showing Off on Dates** - Whilst it's nice to be wined and dined if you notice that your partner goes out of their way to basically show off when they take you out, it could be a narcissistic nod. Do be careful with this one, because it could equally be your partner trying to woo you! A few signs to look out for include tipping far too much, not tipping at all, treating the waiter with disrespect, or ignoring advice on wine/food from the waiter and telling them that he/she knows better.

- **Always Breaks Promises and Oversteps Boundaries** - If he or she is always borrowing things and not bringing them back, maybe borrowing money, or simply avoiding the need to recognize your personal boundaries, then that is a narcissist sign to look for. A narcissist doesn't have respect for anyone else's thoughts or feelings, because they have very little empathic ability. They also don't know much about personal space, so if you find that they're always 'in your space', that's something to look out for too. If they make you a promise and barely keep it, again, red flag.

- **Everything is Your Fault** - They make you a promise or say they'll do something and when they don't do it, they turn the blame onto you. For example, perhaps you were supposed to meet for coffee after work but he or she didn't turn up. A response could be 'what do you expect, you didn't remind me!'. They might be cooking dinner and burn it, and it will be your fault because you distracted them with something you said.

- **They're Always Looking in The Mirror** - Whilst many men and women have slight vanity issues, narcissists are literally in love with their own appearance. If you notice that your partner is always looking in the mirror, always changing their hair or dress sense to look good and gain approval from others, then narcissism could be on the cards. A narcissist has to be the best, look the best, and be admired, and they place a huge amount of importance on appearance over everything else.

- **Your Opinion Isn't Worth Anything** - If you're having a conversation about something and you voice your opinion, a true narcissist will belittle that view and tell you that you're stupid/your opinion is stupid/tell you that theirs is better. Trying to get a narcissist to agree with you is a blatant waste of time and oxygen.

- **They Have to Have the Best** - Possessions and the way others see them is vital to a narcissist. For example, if you're trying to buy a car together but you're on a budget, a narcissistic would rather go down the finance route and land themselves in debt to drive the latest Mercedes, than go for something lower in status quality, but within budget.

- **They Matter, You Don't** - A narcissistic partner will expect you to forget your wants and needs and focus entirely on theirs. If anything, your wants and needs never registered on the scale! You will, therefore, need to drop everything for what they need, and they will not show any thanks in return.

- **Arguments Often End in Them Sulking or Running Away** - Narcissists do not handle rejection or criticism well, in fact, it will end in them either sulking and starting another argument or running away/becoming emotionally detached. This can extend to a certain type of emotional abuse also because by belittling you in the middle of an argument, they make themselves feel better about the criticism you've given them (probably rightly).

- **They Often Act Out of Jealousy** - Narcissists are often quite jealous and this is even more so in a relationship. If you notice regular bouts of jealousy, then that is a narcissistic red flag to be aware of.

How many of those signs you see in your relationship depends on whether or not you can truly class your partner as narcissistic. Don't go throwing the label around just because you can tick off one or two! Remember, in order for a narcissist to be diagnosed with NPD, they need to tick five or more of the traits from a rather short list, as outlined in the diagnostic criteria. We can't give you a definite number of these signs to tick off, but you would be looking at half or more, over a constant period of time, before you could categorically decide either way.

Is There a Future for a Relationship Touched by Narcissism?

Ah, the million-dollar question. We cannot say yes, and we cannot say no, it really depends on the couple and the amount of narcissistic involved.

What one person is happy to put up with, another person would run away from. What you need to do, however, is ask yourself whether you're truly happy and whether you see a future for the two of you. Never stick with a narcissistic person if they are making you feel unhappy, belittled, or questioning your own self-esteem or sanity. The problem is, that questioning your own sanity is part of the whole gaslighting issue we've mentioned so many times already.

Many men and women stay in narcissistic relationships because they aren't sure whether or not they're imagining it, or whether it's really happening. Deep down, they know something isn't right and they know that they shouldn't be dealing with the way things are, but they love that person, and they don't want to give up on them. Whenever their partner shows their bad side, they quickly show their good side not long afterwards; by doing that, they're keeping the person right where they want them - not leaving.

In terms of whether there is a future or not, perhaps we should instead be questioning whether there is a *healthy* future or not. There is a difference between a general future and a healthy one. A relationship where one partner is constantly belittling and dragging down another isn't healthy, whether they're doing it because of a personality disorder or not.

There aren't that many narcissists who remain in relationships for that long. The reason is that in the end, the other partner really sees the light and finds the strength to leave. This doesn't always happen, and there are instances where a future could be on the cards, provided the narcissistic partner is able to realize that they are doing and get help. It does happen, but it doesn't happen often.

Whilst we might be painting a bleak picture, it really is a case of looking at your individual circumstances and deciding what is right for you. There is no right or wrong answer here.

The Narcissist and The Empath

There is one particular toxic mixture that we need to talk about in more detail. This combination of people is a highly damaging and extremely incompatible one, but it is also a very common union you will find. We are talking about a person classed as an empath and a narcissist of any type.

For this to be a damaging combination, the narcissist doesn't have to be a toxic or malignant type, they can be classic, vulnerable, or a combination of types. The problem here is that an empath is an extremely sensitive person, someone who is hurt easily and who wants to help. A narcissistic possesses very little, probably zero, empathy and as a result, the two cannot understand each other. You might wonder in that case how they come together in the first place, but it is a union which is surprisingly common.

The bottom line is that an empath wants to help, and they are attracted by the charming nature of a narcissist when they first meet. Whilst empaths usually have extremely good instincts and can normally spot someone acting out of character from a long distance, a narcissist is extremely good at getting past that defense mechanism. As a result, the empath finds themselves totally enamored with this new person in their lives. They then start to see chinks in their armor, e.g. the vulnerable side, the side which needs constant reassurance. The empathic side of their nature then wants to help, and almost wants to 'fix' the narcissist.

As we've explored already and will certainly delve into in more detail later in the book, a narcissist cannot be fixed, as this is an ingrained part of their personality which requires professional assistance in order to change the disordered pattern of thinking. What eventually happens is that the empath is belittled and emotionally damaged by the narcissist's lack of empathy and general behavior. It's also likely to be the case that an empath will struggle to leave the narcissist because they will keep turning on the charm just at the moment, they think the empath is finally going to summon up the courage move on.

Empaths are extremely sensitive, as we have already said. They do not understand how someone can use emotions for manipulation and they are extremely easy to hurt. Therefore, the thoughtless actions of a narcissist can cause extreme upset and hurt to an empath.

Of course, the same could be said for any type of emotionally sensitive person. In many cases, narcissists actually seek out vulnerable and sensitive people, because they are far easier to manipulate. This is particularly the case with toxic and malignant narcissists, who almost seem to get a kick or some kind of enjoyment out of causing distress and upset to another person.

Unfortunately, the only way to get around this particular problem is for an empath to see the light and leave. For many people, however, that is extremely difficult and pulls on every heart string possible. Even when someone does bad to an empath, they still try and see the good in them.

When it's Time to Leave

Whilst it's not impossible for a relationship touched by narcissism to succeed over time, there are far more instances when the union will ultimately fail. It is likely to be a long and protracted process, because of something which we're going to finally get around to discussing next - gas lighting.

The person in the relationship with the narcissist will question themselves endlessly and wonder whether they really are being treated badly, or whether they are imagining it. The narcissist will turn everything around on them and make them feel like it's them that is to blame. For a person who is quite sensitive or emotionally vulnerable, this type of treatment can cause them to stay in a relationship which is damaging and unhealthy for far too long.

A person leaving a narcissistic relationship will probably go back a few times before finally breaking contact. A narcissist is unlikely to just 'let it go'. As we've mentioned previously in this book, many narcissists want to have the best of the best, and they collect things as possessions. In some ways, their partner is an extension of that. When their partner chooses to leave them, they see this as a failure and a huge rejection. They will react either with anger, or they will attempt to charm them back, reverting to the 'old' version which initially attracted the person to them in the first place. In many cases, this can be enough to get their partner to return to them because they still have deep feelings underneath it all.

Many partners who leave this type of relationship require a large amount of support afterwards, and some even require emotional counseling. Depending upon the type of treatment they have been subjected to (far worst in the event of being close to a toxic or malignant narcissist), the empath may find it extremely difficult to have trusting and healthy relationships in the future, without some kind of therapy or support into the future.

As you can see, narcissistic relationships aren't just damaging for the narcissist (because many ends up missing out on genuine loving unions as a result of their inability to have healthy relationships), but also for the partner too. Leaving it difficult, and in some cases, it can be a process which takes months, if not years.

It's often the case that they know their partner is narcissistic towards the end. This is usually the catalyst for making them think they should leave. However, when gas lighting begins, the difficulty really turns itself up a notch or two.
So, let's finally get around to it - what is gaslighting?

Understanding Gas Lighting

First, let's define the term.

To gaslight or gas lighting, is to psychologically manipulate someone into doubting their own sanity.

This is a classic narcissistic move, and it is something which all types of narcissists use from time to time. It can be mild, moderate, or it can be extremely severe. In the case of being emotionally abused by a toxic or malignant narcissist, gas lighting can cause the partner to feel like they are actually going insane.

To really highlight what gaslighting is in practice, let's look at some of the classic techniques used by narcissists, which all add up to the same thing - gas lighting.

• **Withholding** - The narcissist will refuse to listen to their partner or pretend that they simply don't understand what they're saying. They will do this by twisting things, e.g. 'here we go again, you just keep saying the same things', or 'I have no idea what you're talking about'.

- **Diverting or blocking** - This can include telling their partner that they're simply imagining it, that it's not happening and they're creating it in their head. It can also include changing the subject so that their partner doesn't get a chance to air their problem or views. For instance, 'you're imagining it'.
- **Countering** - In this case, the narcissist will make the partner question their memory of something that happened, even though they have it perfectly clear in their own mind. For instance, 'you never remember things properly, that didn't happen'. The partner then starts to question whether it really did happen or not.
- **Denial** - This is when the narcissist will make their partner question whether something really did happen. This is likely to be the case when the narcissist promised to do something and didn't. Rather than admitting that they forgot, they will say 'I don't know what you're talking about', and pretend it never happened.
- **Trivializing** - This is a common form of emotional belittling, whereby the narcissist places no importance on the way their partner feels, or their needs. For instance, 'you're far too sensitive'. 'I can't believe you're upset about something that small'.

These five techniques are classic gaslighting methods, and they can be used all at once, in separate sequences, etc. How a narcissist uses gas lighting entirely depends on the situation, but they all add up a form of emotional manipulation which can, in the end, cause the partner to stay with them when they deep down know they should leave; this happens because the partner starts to wonder whether it really is them making things up and seeing things that aren't there, or whether their instinct is right. The doubt is often enough to make them stay but remain unhappy.

It's important that your understanding of gas lighting is really clear because this type of emotional manipulation really adds up to abuse. It's so subtle that a person often doesn't realize they're being subjected to it. If you're not sure if this is happening to you, ask yourself the following questions:

- Do you constantly doubt yourself, always second-guessing?
- Do you ask yourself if you're too sensitive on a regular basis?
- You feel confused on a regular basis, and sometimes wonder if you're going crazy
- You're always the one saying sorry, even though you sometimes think you shouldn't apologize
- You know that you're unhappy and you can't really understand why
- You're always trying to make excuses for the behavior of your partner to those close to you, e.g. friends or family
- You often don't tell your friends and family about things that have happened
- You have a gut feeling something isn't right, but you have far too many doubts to act upon it
- You start to pull yourself back and act in a different way, even lying, to avoid situations which you know are going to be twisted

- You look back on the past fondly, remembering when you were far more fun-loving and relaxed
- You often feel that you can't do anything right
- You start to question your ability to be a good partner

If you're thinking these things on a regular basis, there is a very good chance that you are a victim of gaslighting by a narcissistic partner. The importance of recognizing this is so great that we can't emphasize it enough. People who are being emotionally manipulated in this way cannot see it because gas lighting is very successful. It is subtle enough to go undetected but strong enough to work.

Let's further reinforce this subject with a few signs that you are in a relationship with a narcissistic partner, who is using gas lighting as a manipulation technique.

- **They lie a lot, to your face** - You know they're lying, but the lies are so blatant that you can't help but wonder whether it's a truth. This is about keeping you off-balance, so you are never really sure what the truth is.
- **They always deny that they said something, even though you know they did** - Even if you have a text message from them saying a specific something, they will deny it and even deny the proof exists. It starts to make you question reality too. The more they do it, the more you start to believe that their side of the story is right.
- **They use those close to you** - A narcissist might use your family and friends, those they know are important to you, and

say nasty things to damage your self-esteem. For instance, if you have children, they might turn around and say: "you shouldn't have had your children you're not a fit mother". This means their emotional attack hits deep.

- **You can see the pattern over a long period of time** - Gas lighting never happens quickly, and it is always a long, drawn-out process which digs deep over time. It will start slowly, e.g. the odd lie or remark, and then it will gain momentum. The fact it starts in this way means that a partner will rarely notice it until they are in the grips.
- **They don't do as they say** - The whole 'actions speak louder than words' analogy is clear here. If you can look at what your partner is saying and see that it doesn't match what they are doing, this is a subtle gaslighting technique. Remember that words mean nothing if they're not backed up by reinforced actions.
- **They use positive words and actions too** - If someone was gaslighting you on a negative level all the time, you would see it; in this case, a narcissist will revert back to their old charming self, and compliment you, to confuse you into thinking that you're imagining all the bad things. For instance, they will belittle you and make you feel worthless about an opinion or something you did, and then they will praise you for something else. This means that the power balance is always in their favor, and they know that confusion is always going to be an element in you staying and not leaving them.
- **They tell other people you're crazy, or you** - If your partner is always telling you that you're crazy, or they tell

other people that you are, that is gas lightning because it's surely going to make you question your own sanity.

- **They make you believe that everyone else is lying, or to blame** - This is another method to make you question your own sanity and wonder who is actually telling you the truth. The end result is probably that you alienate yourself from those around you, and the only person you have is the narcissist themselves.

The main point of highlighting these common examples is to help you quickly become aware of whether or not a narcissist is actually gaslighting you. See how many of these you can nod your head to. Remember, it's not a definite sign of gas lighting if you can only tick one off, and it only happened once. Everyone is a little manipulative from time to time, it's part of human nature; however, if it happens on a regular basis and you can agree to several techniques, that could be a very real sign that this form of emotional manipulation is actually happening to you.

We've mentioned that the term 'narcissist' is far too often thrown around these days and that real narcissism is actually rarer than most people think, on the other hand, is extremely common, but we should point out that it's not only used by narcissists. This is a form of emotional abuse which can be used by anyone who wants to manipulate another person. It has roots in narcissism, and most narcissists (all types) use it. Be on the lookout for these types of techniques coming your way and be sure to spot the red flags before they become too ingrained. Remember, it's not your fault, and you're not going crazy.

Dealing with Emotional Abuse

The problem with emotional abuse is that the person who is being abused is often clueless that it is happening. That all comes down to gas lighting, and the fact that the narcissist has used is to so slowly and subtly, that it has crept up on them without them even noticing it. By the time they start to question what is really happening, and perhaps someone else makes them aware of it, getting out of the situation has become very difficult indeed.

Emotional abuse is never okay, and it is not something you should stick around and cope with. The title we have used, i.e. 'dealing with emotional abuse', isn't about coping with it and staying in the same situation, it is about to understand it and getting out of it in a healthy way, to minimize future effects on your emotional and mental health.

Emotional abuse often flies under the radar and isn't given the same amount of shock factor as those who are victims of physical abuse. This is probably because there are no physical scars to see; you can't see the scars that someone inflicts emotionally, they can only be felt. The thing is, physical abuse heals, and whilst it certainly leaves mental scars, finding support is usually an easier process. Society has made it far more difficult to seek help for emotional issues; we tend to recognize what we can see. Hopefully, in the future, that will change, but the tides are turning and there is a lot more recognition of emotional abuse as a damaging factor than ever before.

Over time, emotional abuse can cause a person to question their entire sanity, making them live with cripplingly low self-worth and self-confidence. They will become house-bound, alienating themselves from those close to them and avoiding anything socially minded. This is not a happy or healthy life.

The following steps will help you deal with the emotional abuse that a narcissistic relationship may be throwing your way.

- **Identify What is Really Happening** - First things first, you need to be honest with yourself and see things for what they truly are; you are being emotionally abused by a narcissist. Yes, you may love this person, but this relationship is not healthy for you, and you are the main concern here, right now.
- **Make Your Own Health a Priority** - Your mental and physical health should be the most important thing on your mind right now. Stop trying to please your partner, and instead turn your attention inwards. Make steps towards increasing your confidence, perhaps by finding a new hobby or starting the gym and boosting your health and confidence. Practice self-care and allow yourself to heal, before making positive, affirmative steps.
- **Set Yourself Boundaries** - It's vital that you set boundaries with your partner. Tell them that they cannot shout at you like that, they can't insult you, they can't call you names. You should also tell them that if they continue to do this, you will leave. If they do it again, simply walk out of the room. It's vital that you follow through on these boundaries.
- **Stop the Blame Game** - Anyone who has been subject to emotional abuse at the hands of a narcissist will probably

send a large proportion of their day blaming themselves for everything that goes wrong in the relationship. This needs to stop. Ask yourself this very painful, but very real question - why would someone who claims to love you act this way? Yes, they have a condition, but does this mean you have to suffer? No. You cannot control the situation, so avoid blaming yourself for it.

- **Be Very Clear in Your Own Mind That You Cannot Fix Them** - Do your research into NPD and be very clear that you cannot fix them, so don't even try. You can attempt to have a conversation with them and perhaps highlight the fact that you suspect they may have NPD, but a true narcissist is probably going to throw that idea right out of the window and blame you for suggesting it. You're going around in circles and it's time to break the chain.

- **Build up a Network of Support** - Confide in someone you trust about the reality of your situation and do not feel ashamed or guilty about it. The more support you can muster, and it is out there, the easier it will be for you to gain perspective and become strong enough to make your final step.

- **Walk Away** - Sounds easy, but it's not in practice. Put together a plan which allows you to walk away from this abusive relationship with your head held high. Know in your heart that your partner will try to pull you back, but that is the whole point of putting together the support network we mentioned in our last step. Be strong and know that you do not deserve to be abused, by someone who has a condition or otherwise.

- **Seek Help if You Need it** - It's not a weakness to ask for help, and if after you've finally broken the relationship you need to speak to a professional in order to work through the issues you've faced, then do it. Most people who have been in these types of relationships do need some kind of therapy or counseling afterwards, in order to build their self-confidence and sense of self-worth once more. By doing this, you're investing in your future, when you meet someone who truly does deserve your kind heart.

The hardest thing about NPD is that it is a personality disorder and therefore a mental health condition. We know that a person doesn't do this by choice, but they also don't choose to seek help and fix it either. Know 100% that there is nothing you can do, know that you deserve better and that although you love this person, they are never going to be what you really need and deserve.

Why Narcissists Are Often Lonely People (Although Won't Admit it)

The fact that we've spoken in detail about the fact that a person in a narcissistic relationship will probably need to leave, tells you a lot about why narcissists are often lonely people. The problem is, they won't admit this. They will tell you that the people who have walked out of their lives weren't worthy of their time or attention anyway. Their sense of grandeur stops them from seeing that they treated someone special very badly, or that they perhaps were at fault for them leaving in the first place.

It's a sad fact, but most narcissists end up alone, and those who do go on to have relationships are often poor relationships which aren't at all healthy. Of course, it's not a 100% certainty that a narcissist will be lonely, because some do go on to have brighter futures, but in order to do that they need to seek help and counseling to overcome their personality disorder and be able to, therefore, have healthy and meaningful relationships in their lives, to the benefit of both sides.

Chapter 5
Helping Someone with Narcissism

You might wonder why we are going to talk about how you can help someone with narcissism when we have spent so long telling you that you can't fix them. That isn't the point. We're not suggesting that you can wave a magic wand and fix this person, allowing them to have meaningful and lasting relationships and friendships, we're suggesting that there are ways you can at least help someone, and maybe encourage them seek help.

Know right now that it might not work - narcissists are by their very nature very stubborn and are not going to accept help if they don't deem it to be strictly necessary. By suggesting that they may have a problem and need help, you are (in their eyes) attacking their very personality and self, and that will not be taken lightly.

Narcissists aren't always 100% narcissistic; you might have someone who only has narcissism when certain events trigger it, e.g. when they're rejected or go through a hard time, and as a result, their personality disorder comes to the fore. On the other hand, you might deal with someone who is narcissistic all of the time, but not to a huge degree. These are the types of people you may be able to help, but anyone who is 100% severe and toxic in terms of narcissism, don't even bother trying to help. These people will not take your suggestion well, and the only way that these types of narcissistic will ever receive help is when they take everything a step too far.

How Can You Help a Narcissistic Person?

So, in what ways can you actually attempt to help a narcissistic person?

There are very few ways you can change anything, but you can try and encourage them to seek help by subtle moves. Again, this depends on the type of narcissism they are experiencing. You should also be very prepared for rejection of your point but know that at least you tried. From there, you can figure out your own options and decide what your own plan of action is going to be. Remember, you can't change someone else without their will to want to change, you can only control yourself.

There are three main ways you can attempt to help someone close to you who is clearly in the grips of NPD.

Do Not Allow Them to Manipulate You

This particular step is for you mainly, but it does help them indirectly. By refusing to let them manipulate you, by allowing their gaslighting attempts to backfire, you're actually making them sit up and take notice. They will see that you are stronger, and they will wonder why. They will not want you to leave, they need you around, even though their behavior probably shows otherwise.

Of course, in order to not let them manipulate you, you need to be aware that emotional manipulation is going on in the first place. The steps we talked about in our last chapter, in terms of how to deal with emotional abuse, will help you in this regard. Set boundaries and tell them that the way they are speaking to you isn't acceptable and that you will simply walk away when they do it. In addition, make sure if you say you're going to do something, you actually do it.

In some ways, dealing with a narcissist is like dealing with a child. If you tell them they can't have something, but then give in, they'll simply continue that level of behavior because they know you'll give in at some point. Narcissists will do the same thing, which is why it is so important that if you say you're going to walk out of the room when they belittle you, you actually do it. Do not apologize for something that isn't your fault and do not bow down to their demands.

This will take practice and it will be hard, but by looking after yourself and your own needs first, you will find the strength to be able to do it.

By ensuring that their tactics backfire, you're taking away a huge amount of their power. This could go one of two ways - they could turn angry and simply lash out at your attempts, or they could possibly start to soften. It depends on the level of narcissism they are affected by. Of course, if they lash out, cut your losses and walk away. You've tried, and there's nothing more you can do.

Wait Until They Are Calm, And Have a Discussion

If you've tried step one and it didn't go too badly, e.g. they soften a little, then perhaps this second step may help. Remember, in order for someone to seek help, it has to be their decision. It's no good forcing someone to see a doctor for anything they don't believe is wrong with them. Think about an alcoholic, for instance, you can't force them to see a doctor and admit that they need help - the first step towards recovery is knowing that there is a problem in the first place.

The types of treatment for NPD all hinge on total commitment to the treatment at hand. If someone doesn't really believe they need this help, the treatment isn't going to work at all. So, the point of this step is to simply sew a seed in their mind and help them explore the possibilities.

Wait until they are calm and sit down and have a conversation. Be soft and don't be forceful. Talk to them, not at them, and make sure that you keep your emotions level. Tell them that you feel like they're treating you in an unfair way and give examples to back up your words. Tell them that you know they don't mean to treat you this way and that they are a good person. If they remain calm, you may be able to make progress. If they simply throw a narcissistic tantrum and turn it around, again, you can't do anymore.

Find some literature on NPD and leave them on the table. Tell them that you've found this information and perhaps they might like to read it. Suggest you can read it together, or they can read it on their own, and that you'll be by their side whatever they decide.

Remember, it's not 100% guaranteed that this step will work, but it's worth a try if you want to know you did all you could before you decide whether or not to walk away. It's also important that if by some stroke of luck, they do agree to perhaps talk about things with a health professional, and that they recognize there might be something not quite right, then you remain supportive and on their side at all times. Remember that deep down a narcissistic is lacking on confidence and needs constant reassurance. The fact that you've suggested there might be something wrong with them could go either way, but by being soft and supportive, being on their side at all times, you may be able to guide them through it and towards professional help.

Issue an Ultimatum

This is the final method to try, and it's not one you should attempt as a first port of call. This is not likely to go well, but there is a chance. By issuing an ultimatum you're basically saying 'look, I do not want to be treated in this way, but I know it's now what you really mean to do deep down. I'm giving you one chance to sort this out, and I will be by your side all the way. If you refuse, and if you continue to act in this way, I will leave for good'. You have to go through with your ultimatum and do not attempt to go back on it. Be strong and see it through, whichever way it goes.

The point of this, however, is not to shout and lecture, it's a firm statement of intent. If you add emotions and hysterics, they are not going to take you seriously.

These are the only ways you can attempt to help someone with NPD, without actually being a health professional. Even if you were a health professional, the person would need to be willing to seek help and make a commitment towards really putting in the effort to change. Treatment for NPD is quite intensive and requires a lot of deep thinking and behavior change. This requires a strong will to make it work, so you can see why someone who is being forced to seek help is not going to have a good outcome.

The Importance of Knowing You Cannot "Save" Anyone

We've said this once, and we need to say it again. You cannot 'save' a person with NPD, and you cannot fix them. This intention can only come from themselves. It's sad to walk away from someone who has a condition and doesn't actually 'mean' to act in a certain way, but at the same time, you can't wave a magic wand and make it all go away again either.

The only thing you can do is focus on yourself and go with what you feel is right. You know in your gut that you deserve happiness and if your partner/friend or whoever this person is to you is not going to give you that, the only thing you can do for yourself is walk away. If you are in a relationship with this person, what would happen if children came into the equation? Would you want them to be born into a relationship that had a large narcissistic element? That is certainly something to think about too.

Make sure that you have this fact in your mind before you attempt to help someone with NPD, and before you make a decision to walk away. By knowing that in a solid and firm manner, you won't have regrets about your final actions.

Are Narcissists Dangerous?

The final thing to address in this chapter is to talk about whether narcissists are actually dangerous people.

The answer to this is wide-ranging and it really depends on the person. Is a toxic or malignant narcissist dangerous? Yes. Perhaps not physically so, but certainly emotionally dangerous and mentally abusive. This type of narcissistic has no problems with manipulating another person; to give you an idea of how bad this can get, a toxic narcissist will stand there and laugh when their partner is having an emotional breakdown and crying because of something they've said or done. These types of narcissists are cruel, so in that way, yes, they are dangerous; dangerous to someone's mental and emotional wellbeing.

Dangerous physically? We can't generalize but on the whole, no. Having said that, toxic narcissists are sometimes linked with psychopaths and sociopaths, and there are many triggers which can send that type of person over the edge and towards extremely dangerous behavior.

If we're talking about a classic or vulnerable type of narcissist, the danger is more likely to be subtle and emotional, rather than physical. Remember, emotional abuse is just as bad (if not worse) than physical abuse, and just because you can't see the scars, it doesn't mean they're not there.

Dangerous for your future happiness? Definitely.

Chapter 6
After You Walk Away

If you do have to walk away from a narcissistic partner, friend, family member, etc., then there are a few things you need to know about 'after the event'.

It's this simple - a narcissist is not likely to shrug his or her shoulders and say, 'okay then, see you', and then let you walk away with nothing else occurring. It's far more likely that they will revert to their best behavior and try and lure you back.

There is one very good reason for this - because they hate rejection and take it very badly indeed. When you walk away from a narcissist you are rejecting them as a person, no matter how badly they treated you. They will not see all the emotional abuse and manipulation that came your way, in their eyes, they treated you like a king or queen. Instead, they will see you walking away, and it will rile them, or cut deep into their self-conscious depths. The next step could be one of two things:

- They will either become angry and resentful and probably bombard you with messages and social media posts about how they're better off without you and you're this, that, and the other (more abuse)
- Or they all become the epitome of charm once more and try and remind you of all the good times

If you find scenario one coming your way, ignore and block. This is simple pride getting in the way. In this case, they see you as rejecting them, they see you as making a mistake, and they're turning the whole thing on you. Of course, you know better. Block their number, block them on social media, do not go anywhere you know they will be, and go and stay with a friend for a while if you're worried, they're going to turn up at your door. Eventually, they will become bored and grow tired with no response. Sad, but true.

Scenario two is also common, and this is how many people in narcissistic relationships end up going back time and time again. The only answer here is to stand firm and remember why you left. If you can stick with your tried and tested support group, then even better. These people will remind you when your resolve might be wobbling, and it will at some point. You did have good times, and you were with them for a reason. Remember, if you've been a victim of gaslighting then it might also be that you're unsure of your next step because you're still suffering from the after-effects of this type of emotional abuse. Your friends and family will need to hold you firm in this case, but again, block numbers and social media access. The less they can contact you, the easier it will be for you to make large strides into your future.

What to Expect:
- Begging
- Pleading
- Bargaining
- Blame games

- Insults
- Eventual silence

If you think you're out of the woods then the silence comes, don't be so hasty. If they see you in the street quickly afterwards, bargaining and pleading is likely to start again. Breaking away from a narcissist takes time but know that it will be a process you'll be pleased you embarked on.

Dating After Leaving a Narcissist

Once you are over the 'getting away from a narcissist' process, the future will seem brighter and far clearer. It's important to give yourself the time to grieve the relationship properly, and not to jump straight into another union in order to try and block out the upset that occurred previously. This is a common scenario, but more common is trying to avoid another relationship altogether.

Remember that you cannot judge a future partner based on what you went through before, but it's entirely normal if you do. For this reason, seeking out counseling or therapy after leaving a narcissistic partner is a good idea. By not dealing with everything that happened, you are actually putting your future at risk. Many people who have emerged from narcissistic relationships are so scarred by what they went through emotionally, they don't want to ever get close to another person again. As soon as a new partner starts to show even the tiniest hint of something which could be akin to narcissism, they run.

The fact is that we all show slight signs of narcissism from time to time, but that doesn't make us narcissists. We can all lack empathy sometimes, we can all belittle someone without meaning to once or twice, and we can all act in ways we wish we hadn't. The difference is that we will apologize and see the error of our ways, whilst a narcissist won't. Do not make the error of labelling everyone with the same tag or tarring everyone with the same brush.

The best way to dip your toe back into the dating world after emerging from a narcissistic relationship is to do so slowly. Try this:

- Give yourself time to simply be. Don't attempt to do anything, don't try and feel anything and don't push yourself to move on; simply spend time on yourself and try and unpick the events in your mind and deal with them. If you need to gain someone else's perspective, or you need to seek out professional help, now is the time to do so.
- Focus on yourself. Next, it's time to seek out things you enjoy and be kind to yourself. You spent so long with someone being unkind to you, it's likely that you've forgotten how to do things for yourself and to enjoy them. Find a hobby you've always wanted to try, go to a night class, go out with friends, spend Sunday mornings being lazy, read your favorite books, eat your favorite foods, and get out into nature.
- Focus on your health. Next up, after your self-focusing time, turn your attention to your health. A healthy body and mind are the best types of revenge! Whilst revenge shouldn't be on your mind, being a better version of yourself after a bad

experience certainly feels great. Eat healthy foods, make sure you get plenty of exercise, get plenty of sleep, avoid stress, and make sure that you challenge your mind on a regular basis. You will notice how much stronger you feel.

- Enjoy your life. Once you start to feel better, and it may take considerable time in some cases, simply start to enjoy your life. Don't make it your sole aim to meet someone, and don't even think about dating; if it happens, it happens. There is plenty of time for all of that.

- When you're ready, simply be open to the possibility. The point is to try and meet someone who is worthy of your time and attention and who can give you what you didn't have before. The point isn't for someone to complete you or heal you. When you think you might be ready, simply be open to meeting people, but don't place huge importance on it. People who have come out of narcissistic relationships can sometimes be needy because they're so desperate for it not to happen again. By following these steps and placing importance on building yourself up once more, this is far less likely to happen to you.

- Do not tar them with the same brush. Again, if you do meet someone and you start to date, don't tar them with the same narcissistic brush as your ex. This is a vitally important step. True narcissists are very, very rare, and that is something to remember. It's highly unlikely you're going to meet someone with NPD twice in your lifetime, and whilst it's possible that you might meet someone who acts a little narcissistic on occasion, this isn't at rue narcissist and therefore won't bring the same types of problems.

- Know the signs. Do not run at the first sign of a problem but always hold your requirement for respect and understanding high up on your list. If someone starts to treat you badly, address the issue and stand firm before walking away. If being in a relationship with a narcissist will teach you anything, it's not to allow the same thing to happen again.

If you're reading this and thinking 'there's no way on Earth I'm even attempting to date again, I'm good by myself', it's time to question why you feel that way. Are you saying that because you truly don't want a relationship and you would rather be alone and spend your time traveling, making meaningful connections with friends, etc? Or, are you saying it because you're scared of going through the same thing twice?

Some people don't want to be in a relationship and that's fine, provided it's for the right reasons. If you're avoiding romantic connections simply because you're scared, that's something to address early on. You will probably find that your feelings change over time, but avoid being closed off to possible connections, simply because your past experiences are clouding your judgement.

Remember, you deserve to be loved, no matter what you might have been forced to believe in the past.

The Future for a Narcissist Who Refuses Help

We've talked a lot about the future for a person who was in a narcissistic relationship, but what about the future for the narcissist themselves?

It doesn't paint a great picture if the person isn't willing to seek help. In that case, it's far more likely that a narcissist will end up jumping from destructive relationship to destructive relationship, and if they do end up in a long-term union, it's unlikely that their partner will be truly happy and fulfilled. That person is far more likely to be simply 'putting up' with the narcissism.

If a narcissist ends up in a relationship which yields children, the sad truth is that their children are quite likely to develop narcissistic tendencies as a result of being open to them during their early years. Whilst there isn't a certain answer in terms of what causes NPD, there a definite suggestion that childhood experiences have a very firm link towards someone developing the personality development in their adolescent and then adult years.

Narcissists also have a habit of becoming quite bitter over time. This is partly because people have come into their lives and then left them, and they can't see why; of course, they will project the blame onto the other person and won't see their role in them leaving. Many narcissistic traits, therefore, worsen with age, as more experiences are racked up throughout life.

As you can see, it's quite a bleak picture we're painting and that is the sad truth about life as a narcissist. People will only stand being treated a certain way for so long before they eventually pluck up the courage to leave. Whilst some may never get to that point, these relationships are likely to be empty and lacking in true love and respect.

For these reasons, the biggest price a narcissist pays for their actions over time is loneliness and a lack of truly meaningful relationships in the end. For a narcissistic, however, the most loving and deep relationship they have is with themselves.

Are Modern Social Elements to Blame?

You're almost at the point where you know everything there is to know about Narcissistic Personality Disorder and the traits and issues which go alongside it, but we also need to explore one possible area before we sign off. Are modern social elements to blame for the rising number of narcissists in the world?

Remember, true narcissists are quite rare, yet it's a term that we hear on such a common basis. For that reason, perhaps narcissistic tendencies are becoming more common, and we have to question why that is. Is it down to the social pressures we are forced to deal with? Is it down to social media? Is it because of pressures to be the best, look the best, and own the best?

It's probably unfair to lay the blame of narcissism at the feet of modern society, but you have to wonder whether it has played a hand. For instance, social media has made us all so much more aware of other peoples' lives, and our appearances. Social media influences are always telling us that if we want to be the best, we need to look the best, and that means using this product. We're bombarded with people taking selfies and full body photos, without realizing that they've been photoshopped and filtered to within an inch of their lives. Most of what we see these days simply isn't real. Is it any wonder that we have such high and unrealistic expectations of what we're supposed to be, what we're supposed to look like, and what we're supposed to aim for?

We aren't entirely sure what causes NPD, so could it be the things we're exposed to in modern life? Of course, much of NPD is thought to be down childhood experiences, but what influences those experiences? What causes a person to act a certain way, causing trauma to another, which could then lead them to develop a specific type of personality disorder? It's hard to pinpoint, but you have to consider the possibility if nothing else.

Whilst we may never entirely understand what causes NPD, and there will always be a certain amount of stigma attached to it, trying to be the best is always a fruitless task. Perhaps instead we should simply be aiming to be ourselves.

In terms of future generations, perhaps it is our responsibility to ensure that children are raised to be happy with who they are, without the need to continually compete and reach certain unrealistic goals. By doing that, we will raise a generation of youngsters who are well-mannered, respectful of others and fulfilled. Surely those are major boosts towards avoiding personality disorders and the types of trauma which may contribute towards development.

Conclusion

And there we have it! We've reached the end of our book about narcissism, and by now you should be far clearer about what it is and what it really means.

After reading this book you should bandy around the idea of narcissism far less and appreciate that it is actually a truly rare personality disorder which shouldn't be misinterpreted. A person who is a little jealous or unkind once or twice in their life isn't a narcissist, they're simply having a bad day; provided they realize this and apologize to those they offended or hurt, there is no harm done. If however, that person doesn't see a problem with their actions, you could be dealing with someone who has an NPD touch.

Whilst a narcissistic cannot actually 'help' what they do, that doesn't mean that you should stick around and put up with it if they're not willing to seek out help to change. Leaving a narcissist behind isn't easy, but it is entirely necessary in order to live a happier life in the future.

The sad thing about narcissism is that whilst we're always talking about it in a negative way, the person who is truly affected is the narcissist themselves. This person is going to end up lonely unless they seek out steps towards a brighter future. This doesn't happen often however, because most narcissists don't realize there is anything wrong with them, and they assume that everyone else has the problem, not them.

Points to Take Away from This Book

Now you've read everything we've had to say about this rather confusing, yet fascinating subject, what are the main points to take away from the book?

- Narcissism is far rarer than most people think, with just 1% of the population affected on the whole
- True narcissism means being diagnosed with Narcissistic Personality Disorder (NPD)
- Men are far more likely to be narcissistic than women, however, that doesn't mean that female narcissist don't exist!
- A narcissistic is defined by a sense of the grandeur of one's self, inflated ego and self-importance, and a need to be the center of attention, but the traits are quite far-reaching beyond that
- Narcissistic behavior can be mild, moderate, or extremely severe
- Many narcissists use emotional abuse without even realize it, e.g. gas lighting
- There are several types of narcissists, including classic, vulnerable, and toxic
- Toxic or malignant narcissists are extremely damaging and are closely linked to psychopaths and sociopaths
- Many narcissists end up alone in the end, because they refuse to see a problem with their actions, and blame everything on those around them

- A person in a relationship with a narcissist is likely to be subjected to various levels of emotional abuse and manipulation, and will probably find it very hard to leave
- Empaths and narcissists are the worst combinations on the planet
- Treatment for Narcissistic Personality Disorder (NPD) involves therapy, counseling, behavioral therapy and challenging mindsets, and can take a considerable amount of time
- There is no known cause for NPD, however, it is thought to stem from childhood, and could be genetic
- Underneath it all, narcissists are fragile and lacking in self-confidence, with a need for constant validation
- Narcissists take rejection extremely badly
- In order for a person to receive treatment for NPD, they need to realize the problem for themselves, and this cannot be done for them. For this reason, most narcissists are never diagnosed and never treated
- It is impossible to fix or change a narcissist without them seeing the error of their ways and understanding that they have a personality disorder which requires treatment
- Finding the strength to leave a narcissistic relationship can be extremely difficult, and many people need to seek professional help afterwards, e.g. therapy and counseling
- Gaslighting is a very common tool employed by narcissists, which involves manipulating the thoughts and emotions of another person, causing them to question their own sanity
- You should never feel guilty or bad about needing to leave a narcissistic relationship - it's important to focus on yourself

There is a huge amount to talk about on this subject, and we've covered the main areas in detail, whilst reiterating the key points several times. Because narcissism and emotional abuse are so closely linked, this is a subject which requires a lot of press space. There is no fun in being in a relationship with a narcissist, just like there is no fun in a friendship with a narcissist or being closely linked in a working situation. All you will deal with is constantly belittling and their inflated sense of grandeur. Despite that, it's also important to realize that this person isn't a 'bad person', they're someone who is suffering from a personality disorder, which actually links very closely to other mental health problems.

By knowing all you can possibly know about narcissism, you can take the right steps towards managing a situation which is touched by narcissism in your own life.

The takeaway point from this whole book? If a narcissist tells you it's your fault, it's really not. Never feel guilty for putting yourself first.

Extra

If you enjoyed reading this book, please, check the others manuscripts of the author :

Emotional Intelligence

A Complete Guide to Mastering Social Skills, Improving Your Relationships, Controlling your Emotions and Raising Your EQ

Would you like to master social skills and build better relationships? Would you like to improve your communication skills? Would you like to better understand your emotions?

If your answer is yes, this book is what you need!

In today's life, social skills have become more and more important. We often see people with excellent work skills being obscured by others who are less gifted, but who have a better ability to relate to others.

In this complete guide, you will learn all the knowledge necessary to improve your social skills, obtain the desired results in your life and increase the EQ.

You will discover:

- An analysis of emotional intelligence and its aspects
- How to build your emotional intelligence to improve all aspects of everyday life
- How to **improve your motivation** and have a positive attitude
- Practical and feasible **exercises to increase your EQ**
- How to understand your emotions
- Advices on **how to manage stress and anger**
- Causes of everyday problems and how to best deal with them
- How to deal with manipulative people
- **...and much more!**

Every step we take in life, every move that we make is influenced at some point by our emotions. When you find it difficult to manage your feelings, that's when situations start to become a real challenge.

All charismatic and successful people have a great ability to recognize and control their emotions, and therefore maintain the composure needed to make appropriate decisions.

Emotional Intelligence has come to be known as the most important ability for all humans. It can help you in most areas of life. With it, you will be able to build stronger relationships and achieve personal and career goals without getting bogged down by social mistakes and obstacles. Instead, you will be able to avoid such obstacles and learn from your mistakes in social situations. This is all thanks to being aware of yours and others' emotions and the outcomes of certain behaviors.

Victor Murphy

Cognitive Behavioural Therapy

An Effective Guide for Rewiring your Brain and Regaining
Control Over Anxiety, Phobias, and Depression

Suffering from a mental disorder you have probably already
heard about CBT – Cognitive Behavioral Therapy. Even if you
haven't you will learn now how this type of therapy can change
your life. You will finally be able to say goodbye to all those days
when you felt anxious and depressed. Your life will again work
in harmony.

CBT is one of the best tools used by therapies and it is based on
a very simple idea. Because of its simplicity, you can practice

CBT yourself in the comfort of your home. However, in order to do this, you will need this book to guide you through the process.

First of all, you need to get educated about your mental disorder. This will help you to determine how to approach it with more precision. Well, think about it, how can you work on something without first learning about it?

In this book, you will get a simple guide that will help you to use CBT to fight depression, anxiety, and phobias. With patient and everyday work, you will finally win the fight.

Now it is time to stop your negative thoughts, start practice mindfulness so that you can be aware of the sensations happening inside you and in the environment around you. Learn how to form goals and how to organize so that you can achieve them. Goals forming are also the base of good structure CBT session.

So, in this book:

- Introduction to CBT
- How to stop the Negative Thoughts
- Becoming more self-confident
- Forming Goals and achieving them
- Mindfulness as a powerful tool against depression, anxiety, and phobias
- Applying CBT and simple exercises

Victor Murphy

Empath

An Effective Guide to Understanding and Developing Your Gift. Overcome Fears & Use Your Potential

Do you experience countless emotions within the space of one day? Are people always telling you that you're 'too sensitive?' Do you often feel overwhelmed and experience the need to run away from social situations?

If you're nodding your head, there is a very good chance you are an empath.

This is good news! You're one of life's good guys, you're a true Earth Angel, and someone who has massive potential to help others and create a lasting legacy in the world. What you need to do however is learn how to harness that potential and develop your gift.

Empath: An Effective Guide to Finding Yourself and Developing Your Gift is the ideal book for anyone who has empathic tendencies. Not only will you find all the information you need on what an empath actually is, but no stone is left unturned in terms of how to overcome potential challenges and develop your gift to its full potential.

You will discover:

- How to Develop Your Gift

- 7 Reasons Why Being an Empath is a Gift
- Characteristic of Empathic Peoples
- Why Empaths have a Better Ability to Help Others
- How to Use Your Potential
- Quick Quiz to Determine Your Empathic Status

- Spiritual Healing Tools to Help You as an Empath

- **...and much more!**

From learning how to ground yourself to visualization techniques, meditation to self-help, Empath teaches you how to handle the negative energies that come your way, giving you the space to focus on the positives instead.

There is no doubt that being an empath is a challenge, but all it takes is the right information and know how to turn it form a challenging situation, to a hugely positive and special situation instead.

There is no need to be overwhelmed or confused for a second longer, download this book today, and look forward to a brighter future, free of empathic burnout and over-sensitivity.

Victor Murphy

Empath

An Effective Guide to Finding Yourself and Developing Your Gift

By Victor Murphy

Table of Contents

Introduction

All too often we hear buzz words. These are term and words that are over-used in the modern day for a short while, and then they disappear, rarely to be heard of again. These are fashionable terms, things which aren't designed to stick around. Occasionally, however, one of those words does stick around, and it becomes a huge topic of discussion.

For instance, how many times have you heard someone say: 'oh I'm so stressed'? Probably quite a lot. Stress used to be a buzz word, but then society grabbed it and made it part of pop culture. The problem is, these words are used in situations which don't really give them the credit they deserve. Take stress again, for example. When you're truly stressed, it's actually a very serious situation, which could eventually turn out to be life-threatening. Instead, we use that word simply to show that we're feeling a little overwhelmed.

What does all of this have to do with the title of this book, we hear you ask. Empathy and being an empath are others of those buzz words and terms that we hear far too often. Simply because you have empathy for something or someone, it doesn't make you an empath. That is doing a disservice to someone who truly does have this gift.

Now, if you think you are an empath, the fact we're calling it a gift might come as a surprise to you, and you might even become a little angry about it. We're not going to sugar-coat it, being an empath is not an easy task in life, and for most people, it's not even a choice they have. If you're firmly in the negative when it comes to your gift, however, it's simply because you haven't yet unleashed its potential and learned to manage it. In that case, this book is going to be a revelation to you.

The fact you've picked up this book tells us two things - you either think you're an empath and you want to learn more, or you are an empath and you're keen to learn how to channel and control it. Either way, you'll certainly find what you're looking for and more right here.

We're going to give you a breakdown of what it feels like to be an empath so you can figure out one way or another whether this applies to you or not. We're going to tell you the no-holds-barred truth about it too; it's not all roses and sometimes it's hard, but being an empath really is a gift when you break it down - the ability to help others is a truly wonderful thing. What you need to do, however, is learn how to control your gift and to stop it impacting in negative ways on your life.

An empath who hasn't learned how to manage their gift lives a pretty overwhelming and upsetting life. Every single emotion is flying at them every single day, and that can lead to anxiety, depression, and a hell of a lot of stress. Not only that, but they also have to deal with their own genuine feelings too. On the other hand, life for an empath who has learned how to manage and deal with the constant flow of emotions is able to separate things into compartments and as a result, they can use their gift for the general good.

Whether you're an empath or not, this book will give you many hints and tips on how to manage your emotions and perhaps help other people as a result. What you should do however is keep an open mind and give everything we suggest a try. Some suggestions and techniques might not work for you, because we're all individual, but you will not know for sure until you give them a go.

So, enough chat, let's get started on your journey into the deep and wonderful world of being an empathy in the modern day.

Chapter 1
What is an Empath?

You've made it onto our first chapter - that means you're interested and eager to learn more about the world of empathy. Great choice!

Before we really get into the deeper understanding of what it means to be an empath, we first really need to define what an empath is. From there, we need to help you understand whether or not this definition applies to you. If you're not an empath, that doesn't mean this book won't be useful to you. We can all learn new things from different subjects, and it could very well be the case that you have many empathic traits, but you're not 100% empath. Either way, by reading further into the subject, you can perhaps learn to develop your spiritual side and bring your borderline empathic nature further towards the surface.

So, let's put a firm definition on the word 'empath'.

An empath is someone who is sensitive to the emotions and feelings of others.

Now, that could mean a million different things, because we all have an awareness of how someone is feeling simply by looking at their face and reading their body language. The difference for an empath, however, is that they don't simply see and recognize the emotions of another person, they are so sensitive to these emotion vibrations that they begin to take them on as their own.

Let's give an example. If an empath is stood at the bus stop waiting for their bus home from work and there is someone stood next to them who is very angry, it's highly likely that after a short while of being so close to them, the empath will start to feel stirrings of anger too. They have no reason to be angry, and they were perfectly fine before they arrived at the bus station, but their empathic ability has tuned into that person next to them and transferred those emotions.

The angry person may then get on the next bus that arrives, and the empath notices that after a few minutes, the anger subsides and they don't feel it anymore. Instead, another person joins the queue and they are really happy about something which occurred during their working day, they simply can't stop smiling. From being angry ten minutes ago, the empath now suddenly feels uplifted and joyful for no real reason.

This is the up and down world of an empath!

As you can imagine, feeling one emotion after another, and sometimes many all at once can be very exhausting. There are many downsides to having this gift, but it's also very important to point out that there are many advantages too. An empath has the knack of being a true healer, a wonderful listener, and someone who can truly understand others in a way that nobody else can.

Is being an empath a paranormal ability? Nobody really has a firm explanation on the real foundations of such a gift, but it's thought to be more spiritual than paranormal. An empath can't read the future or see ghosts, they are simply extremely attuned and sensitive to other people who are within close proximity to them. They don't have flashbacks and they don't suddenly know why that person is feeling the way they do, they simply feel the emotions as their own.

As you can see, defining the word 'empath' can be very difficult without giving examples to help with understanding!

Being an empath has turned into a rather fashionable label, however, it's far rarer than society will have you believe. What most people confuse is having empathy and being an empath. Let's explore the differences now.

The Difference Between Being an Empath and Having General Empathy

There is a very real difference between having empathy for a person or situation, or generally being a quite empathic person, and being an actual empath. There are links, however, and someone who is very empathic in general may be able to go on to develop their skills towards being an empath.

Let's define the two.

- Empath - Someone who is highly sensitive to the emotions of others and feels them as their own
- Having empathy - The ability to understand and recognize the emotions of another person, but not feeling them as their own

As you can see, the big difference is the transfer of emotions to the point of actually experiencing them as if were their own. A person with empathy is very understanding and quite sensitive to emotions, but they can only experience them as an outsider looking in. An empath, on the other hand, experiences them in very real terms.

Many people confuse the two, and whilst they have similarities, having empathy can be something that is transient, felt from time to time, whereas being an empath isn't really something which can be switched off, it can only be controlled and managed.

You could argue that having empathy is better than actually being an empath, because there is no feeling of the emotions first hand, and therefore none of the associated downsides.

What it Feels Like to be an Empath

You might be reading this and wondering what could be so bad about being an empath. We don't want to paint a negative picture of life as an empath, because once the gift is managed, life can be very bright and helpful indeed. However, when an empathic gift isn't controlled or managed, it can spiral to the point where life is just a constant rollercoaster of emotions.

Think back to a day which was particularly emotional for you. Perhaps a million things went wrong and by the end of the day you'd simply had enough or think of a very emotional situation you dealt with, e.g. perhaps you found out a partner had cheated on you. We'll talk about negative emotions here because these are certainly the most troublesome for an empath - nobody is ever going to complain about feeling many positive emotions!

Once you pinpoint that particularly emotional day, consider how you felt at the end of it. Exhausted probably. You probably wanted to lay down, close your eyes, and forget about everything.

That is what life feels like on a regular basis for an empath who hasn't learned how to manage their gift.
In addition, when you feel something, but you have no idea why you're feeling it, everything is super-confusing too. You might not be able to separate what you're truly feeling for yourself, and what you're feeling in relation to other people. The constant battle between 'is this me, or someone else' can lead towards depression and anxiety, if not handled correctly.

Now, once more we need to highlight that life isn't all bad for an empath. We've painted a rather confusing and torrid time so far, but we need to set the scene of how it will be if you don't learn how to manage it. The thing is, if you can manage it and control it, you will live a very happy and fulfilling life, packed to the rafters with occasions where you can help others and really experience the true joy of knowing that you've possibly helped change someone's life.

Let us tell a quick story to highlight how wonderful being an empath really can be. This is a true story, by the way.

One day, an empath was walking over a bridge. It was a really sunny day and she was feeling light and happy, enjoying her day off. She spotted a man who was stood on the edge of the bridge simply looking down. He had no-one around him, but as she got closer and closer to where he was standing, she noticed her good mood quickly slipping away, and instead a dark cloud came over her. She felt extremely sad, very low, and hopeless. It was a horrible, dark feeling. She knew she was experiencing the man's feelings because she had no reason to feel that way herself.

That man was contemplating suicide because he'd lost his job and he was worried about how he was going to look after his wife and young child. He felt like a failure and was terrified about telling his wife what had happened. He felt like it was easier to jump than to face it.

Do you know what happened next? The empath stood and spoke to the man for a good half an hour. She told him that she knew how he felt. He laughed and asked how on Earth she could understand how he was feeling. She told him that she knew because she felt it, and she told him word for word exactly how he was feeling. The man looked at her in shock. She told him that she understood, and for the first time since the whole ordeal had happened, the man felt like someone really did understand him, and that perhaps the situation wasn't as dire as he had been thinking.

The man didn't jump. He went home, he told his wife, he sought out help financially and whilst things might have been hard for a while, they more than survived.

If that girl, that empath, hadn't felt his emotions and had simply shrugged her shoulders assuming he was enjoying his day and looking out over the bridge at the beautiful scenery, as she had been doing as she'd been walking, perhaps he would have jumped, and that young family would have been ripped apart. Can you see how powerful being an empath can be? It might have its downsides, it might be overwhelming, but those things can be overcome. An empath has the chance to save lives - it's that special.

The 10 Traits of an Empath

Now we know what an empath is, and how it is different from having empathy, let's look at 10 traits of an empath.

Extremely Sensitive

Empaths are very sensitive people, both empathically speaking and within themselves too. An empath is a very spiritually open person and a great listener, they are Earth angels in so many ways, and are very giving people. The downside of being sensitive is that it is easy to become hurt, and empaths, in general, are prone to upset. They do not have tough skins, because their gift requires them to be so open.

Soak up Emotions Like a Sponge

This is the number one trait of an empath, the ability to soak up the emotions of others like a very big sponge! This doesn't only include negative emotions, but positive ones too - they literally feel it all. Empaths can become very tired from being in large groups, because of the sheer number of emotions coming at them from all angles, but when they are within nature and alone, they are peaceful and calm.

Most Have Introverted Personalities
Whilst it's not impossible to find an extroverted empath, you'll find countless more which are introverted and naturally quiet. The reason for this is because most empaths can't cope with large groups or being the center of attention, which most extroverts quite enjoy! Introverts, on the other hand, prefer either being alone or being one on one, which is the perfect situation for an empath. If you do find an extroverted empath, it's likely that they will disappear away from large social situations quite quickly, because they will easily become emotionally overwhelmed.

Extremely Intuitive
In order for an empath to be able to manage their gift and for it not to take over their life, they need to be able to listen to their gut and identify their feelings from those of other people. Being intuitive is very useful for an empath, however, as you will rarely be able to 'pull the wool' over their eyes, and they can usually spot someone who is lying or doing something the shouldn't from a long way away. Empaths are fantastic judges of character.

Often Need Time Alone
In order to deal with the number of emotions they take on every single day, empaths often need time alone. It's very easy to become overwhelmed and drained, and this can manifest both

physically and mentally unless time out is taken. You'll often find empaths driving to wherever they go, even parties, so they can leave easily whenever the situation starts to become a little too much.

May Avoid Relationships

This point is quite a sad one. If an empath hasn't learned how to manage their gift and control it, they may find themselves avoiding romantic relationships. The reason this is sad is that an empath is so sensitive and giving that they are the perfect partner, and they certainly deserve love. The problem is that an empath can easily lose their own identity when they become part of a union, simply because they become so wrapped up in what their partner is feeling and what they're feeling. Taking time out for themselves and having an understanding partner is a way around this. There is no reason why an empath can't have a fulfilling and loving relationship when they learn the techniques and boundaries of controlling their gift.

Often Attract the Wrong Type of People

We're going to talk about this in more detail in a later chapter, but empaths are particularly vulnerable to two types of people - energy vampires and narcissists. Energy vampires are a huge problem for empaths because they simply suck the life out of them and drain their energy. The good news is that an empath's sharp intuition should be able to help them spot these people and avoid them, however, narcissists can be rather clever and dip under the empaths' intuition radar until it's too late. Again, we'll talk about this in more detail shortly.

A True Love of Nature and Quiet
You'll often find an empath outside in nature, walking their dog in the park or somewhere quiet and secluded. Nature is the perfect outlet for an empath, so beaches, mountains, anywhere with water, and plentiful greenery is a place of sanctuary and peace for an empath.

Very Sensitive to Noise and Smells
It's not just feelings that empaths are very sensitive too, but other sensory issues too, such as smells, noises and those who simply talk far too much. Loud noises can be overwhelming, but very strong smells can also be too much for their sensitivity levels. This is another reason why empaths love nature because everything is balanced, and nothing is towards either extreme.

Often a Little Too Generous
Empaths are often a little too generous with their time, simply because they want to help. Remember, an empath is someone who is kind and loving, and this means that they sometimes don't have the right boundaries in place. They can often become very distressed when watching the news, e.g. when seeing bad things going on in the world, but similarly, if a friend is in need, they sometimes don't know how to set boundaries in terms of time spent with their friend and time spent for themselves.

These are the most common traits of an empath, but it may be that you experience your own which are slightly different. It's important to really pinpoint whether you truly are an empath or you're sensitive in general. By knowing this, you'll be able to put into place boundaries and strategies which help you cope with everyday life, and also ways to help you get the most out of your empathic potential. Of course, it may be that you have empathic tendencies, but you really don't want to accept them; in that case, is it possible to fight your natural nature?

Is it Possible to Fight Being an Empath?

Put simply, if you are a true empath, it isn't possible to turn off a switch and not experience the emotions of others as though you were a sponge. What it is possible to do however is control it and be able to minimize the effects.

If you are a person who shows empathy, i.e. you're not an empath but you can easily recognize the emotions of others and appreciate them for what they are, you can turn off the switch. Why you would want to is really a personal deal, but you would simply ignore your instincts until they dumbed down to the point of silence. An empath can't do that. You cannot ignore what you are feeling.

In this case, learning how to embrace and control the gift of being an empath is the only way. It's important to realize that being an empath is part of who you are, and you need to accept it just as you would accept the color of your eyes or the sound of your voice.

Are Empaths Born or Developed?

This is another empath-related question which is asked a lot. Can an empath be developed, or is it a skill which is evident a birth? And, is it an ability which is passed down throughout a family's generations?

Put simply, we don't know!

It's impossible to really measure and study an empath and where the gift comes from because there is no real data which you can collect and do research into. There is a little science behind the brain function of an empath, however, which is really interesting to learn more about. According to Psychology Today, empaths display the following brain-related features:

- **Very responsible mirror neurons** - Studies have revealed a set of cells within the brain which are thought to be responsible for displaying compassion, and also in allowing our brains to mirror the emotions of other people. These calls also allow us to share in another person's feeling, both positive and negative. An empath is considered therefore to have extremely responsible mirror neurons (these special compassion cells), which makes their main function even more enhanced.
- **Sensitive to changes in electromagnetic fields within the body** - Both the heart and the brain have an electromagnetic field, and empaths are thought to be extremely sensitive to changes within them. Both of these fields also give information about the emotions of other people around us, and with a higher sensitivity to these fields, empaths can easily become more overwhelmed than someone with a lower sensitivity.

- **A higher sensitivity to emotional contagion** - Most people experience what is known as emotional contagion. For instance, if someone you love cries, you might start to cry too. Empaths have a higher sensitivity to this issue, and as a result, it is important to pick the people around you very carefully.

- **A higher sensitivity to dopamine** - Dopamine is the neurotransmitter that helps us feel relaxed, content, and happy. Most empaths are very keen to spend time alone, within nature, or generally chilling out; they don't really need a lot to be happy. As a result, a lower amount of dopamine is required. This also backs up why most empaths tend to be introverted, as introverts need less dopamine than extroverts.

These are just a few scientific explanations which may lead us to believe that an empath is far more likely to be born than developed. You can't force these scientific changes within the body. What you can do however is encourage your emotional sensitivity and empathy by being more open to the thoughts and feelings of other people. This will help you show more empathy in your life generally, although it will probably not lead you to take on those feelings as your own, in the case of an empath.

The final point is whether or not being an empath is a gift which is passed down through the generations of a family, e.g. genetic. Again, we don't have a solid yes or no answer, but many people believe that if a parent is an empath, their child is far more likely to also possess the same ability.

Quick Quiz to Determine Your Empathic Status

The fact you're reading this book tells us that you think you might be an empath, or you at least have a large curiosity about it. This final part of our first chapter is going to ascertain your real empathic status. Are you an empath or are you someone who shows a large amount of empathy towards others? Both are fantastic gifts equally.

Firstly, how many of the following personality traits from the following list do you have?

- Quiet
- Thoughtful
- A good listener
- A large heart
- Wants to help
- Often feels tired or overwhelmed when out in public
- Becomes very emotionally attached to the news
- Likes time alone
- Loves nature
- An animal lover
- Often has a lot of headaches which go away after calm time

These are the key traits of an empath. If you have listed at least 8 out of those 11, you are very likely to have an empathic nature. Now, let's do a quick quiz to really pinpoint whether you are an empath, or a very sensitive person (you show empathy easily)

Can you answer 'yes' to 5 or more of these questions:

- I'm often called overly emotional, or told I'm too sensitive
- I find it very easy to cry when watching the news or seeing random acts of kindness
- I often take on the feelings of my closest friends and family, e.g. if my friend is sad, I want to cry
- It's quite easy to hurt my feelings
- When I've been out in a crowd or at a party, I feel tired, emotional, and my body starts to hurt in some way, e.g. headaches or aches and pains
- I often feel happiest when I am alone or with just one other person I know well
- I love animals and feel calm when I am around them
- I avoid romantic relationships because I find them too emotionally taxing
- I often use unhealthy coping mechanisms when I feel overwhelmed or stressed, e.g. I eat too much, I spend money, I drink too much, etc

If you can answer 'yes' to 5 or even more then you are an empath. If you can answer 'yes' to 3 or 4, then you are a very sensitive person who is able to show empathy to those around you.

It doesn't matter which camp you fall into, you still have many things to learn about yourself and the ways to protect yourself from negative energies, whilst also unleashing the power of your special gifts.

Chapter 2
The Threats to an Empath's Peace of Mind

Before we get onto the balancing techniques and the wonderful ways to use your gift, we need to give a special mention to the merry band of people who are out to spoil the party. The first thing you need to realize in your empathic journey is that not everyone is like you - not everyone is kind and open-hearted. We're going to start talking to you as an empath because by getting to this point it's likely that you're more towards the empathic side of the population than otherwise.

There are people out there who are simply negative in general. We're not going to say they're bad people, because most of the time they don't realize that they're actually being negative or causing distress to another, however, some do, and obviously, they are bad people!
There are people who are particularly dangerous or threatening to an empath's peace of mind and general emotional health. Have you heard of narcissists? You probably have, as this is something which many people talk about these days. Narcissists are very dangerous for an empath, and a relationship between a narcissist and an empath is only ever going to end in one way - total heartbreak for the empath. It's really that simple.

There is another type of person you need to be on the lookout for, the energy vampire. We touched upon this subject very slightly in our first chapter, and there are several types of energy vampires to be aware of. We'll cover both of this peace of mind threats in this chapter so you can be more aware of what to look for and avoid like the plague!

Of course, you might be confused because we said that empaths are good judges of character. On the whole, that is true, but narcissists, in particular, are very cleverly disguised. Energy vampires are often mistaken for those in need, who turn out to simply be happy to suck the life right out of you - you've probably met one before, they simply don't stop talking, moaning, and generally being negative. Avoid!

Why Certain People Can be More 'Dangerous' to an Empath Than Others

The word 'dangerous' is probably quite strong, but it is required in some cases. A narcissist, in particular, has the power to emotionally destroy an empath unless they can spot the narcissistic traits quite quickly and take action.

The reason these two groups of people, in particular, are dangerous for an empath's peace of mind is that they feed off of emotions, and those are what an empath thrives on. Remember, empaths are very open-hearted and sensitive people. Human beings are generally quite wonderful, but there are very negative traits possessed by some, e.g. the desire to hurt others, and the desire to take what they can from another person, without really caring about the feelings of the other person. This is a risk for everyone the world over, not just for an empath, but the depth of an empath's feelings means that they are far more likely to be hurt for a longer period of time than someone who doesn't have empathic tendencies.

Heartbreak for an empath can feel like the literal end of the world. Whilst heartbreak is never a good thing in any situation, and can literally be devastating, for an empath it can feel like a complete rejection of every single part of their personality. Why did they do this to me? What is wrong with me? How could they be so mean? What is the point in having feelings like this? These are thoughts that an empath will have after they have been hurt by another person. Their feelings are magnified to the point of being so overwhelming that eating, sleeping, and going about their daily activities can be borderline impossible for a while.

With all of this in mind, it's vital to be able to shield yourself from two specific types of people.

Narcissists and Empaths

This chapter is not designed to be negative, it is designed to be informative, so let's just get that out there now. This particular section is going to be one of the most important you will read, whether you're an empath or you're not. We are all at risk of meeting a narcissist and being totally and utterly devastated by their selfish actions. An empath, however, is likely to be steamrolled by one, and may never be quite so open-hearted again as a result.

Firstly, what is a narcissist?

A narcissist is a person who has the following traits:

- Very selfish
- Everything is about them and they don't care about the thoughts, feelings, or opinions of others - their opinion is the right one and yours is wrong
- A huge sense of self-importance
- Very vain in their appearance
- Always bragging and talking up their achievements
- An overwhelming sense of entitlement
- Often puts down other people or belittles them
- Often needs praise or admiration in order to feel good
- Drags other people down to make themselves feel better

From that, you might think that by meeting a narcissist you're actually meeting the devil. The problem is, narcissists, are far more common than you might think, and the severity of narcissistic behavior can be mild to severe, with several notches in-between.

A trust narcissist actually can't help their actions to some degree, because they suffer from a personality disorder called 'narcissistic personality disorder'. Personality disorders all come under the mental health umbrella, and whilst there are treatment and behavioral therapy available for narcissistic people, it takes acceptance of the problem in the first place. For a narcissist, this is highly unlikely to happen. In the eyes of a narcissist, you're the problem, not them.

To an empath, a narcissist is a true emotional bully. The problem is that narcissists are actually attracted to empaths because of their openness and sensitivity. They falsely see this as a weakness, and an 'in'. Narcissists like to control people because it makes them feel better about themselves and they use a method called 'gaslighting'.

You've probably heard of gas lighting as it has been in the news and in magazines a lot over the last few years. Gaslighting is a form of emotional abuse, which takes the form of causing the person to question their own sanity. For instance, a narcissist will cause so much emotional distress that you start to wonder whether it's them doing it, or whether there is something truly wrong with you. You'll then start to believe that their actions are your fault, e.g. they're shouting at you because you're wrong, or you're creating problems when it's really them doing things they shouldn't. The problem with gas lighting is that it then prevents people from leaving those with narcissist tendencies, who refuse to change, because they're not sure whether they're the one in the wrong or their emotionally abusive partner.

Basically, narcissists play on emotions, and empaths are a huge bundle of emotions.

Can you see how damaging this could be, especially for an empath who hasn't yet learned how to control and manage their gift?

It isn't easy to spot a narcissist, and it doesn't help that there are so many notches in the severity ladder. You might meet someone who is slightly narcissist on occasion, or you might meet someone who is an all singing, all dancing narcissist. You won't know this at first, however, as they will be the epitome of charm and wonder. Their traits won't really come to the fore until you're hooked, completely and utterly under their spell and probably 100% in love with them. Leaving a narcissistic partner takes extreme strength and staying away is even harder because you will always question whether you did the right thing.

For an empath, this is a million times more difficult. How to avoid these people? It's difficult, but being aware of the traits, knowing your own self and being strong is vital. By doing this and knowing what to look for when red flags appear, you can get out of the relationship, or away from the person, before gas lighting and other problematic issues really begin.

Energy Vampires and Empaths

The second issue is less emotionally devastating but no less problematic. The energy vampire.

There are many different types of energy vampires, but they are much easier to spot than a narcissist. You will know if you've met an energy vampire because they will literally suck every little bit of life out of you, hence the name. They will take, take, take, and you'll feel exhausted at the end of it.

A good example of an energy vampire is a person who you have noticed is very down. As an empath perhaps you feel their sadness, so you ask them what is wrong. Big mistake. This person then latches onto you and doesn't let go. They talk, talk, talk, and talk some more. If you have given them your telephone number, that was an even bigger mistake, because they will continue to talk, even when you're not there in person!

As an empath, you're naturally kind and want to help, so it's likely that you'll probably always be there for this person, to listen and offer a shoulder to cry on. What you need to realize is that your self-care and health is just as vital as theirs.

Energy vampires in general lack empathy, which makes them difficult to be around. The other types of energy vampires you need to be on the lookout for are:

- Dominant energy vampires
- 'Playing the victim' energy vampires
- The 'everything is so negative' energy vampire
- Judgmental energy vampires

The list goes on, but these are some of the main types which you need to avoid or minimize your time with. They will exhaust you emotionally and leave you needing to lay down in a darkened room for a time!

The Downsides of Being an Empath

This is the last negative word we're going to say about the whole empathy gift - promise! However, it's important to give a balanced view, and that means the good and the bad. By knowing what to expect, you can better prepare yourself for your embraced life as an empath, and you'll be able to really appreciate the fantastic side of it too - there is one, and we're going to talk at great length about it in our next chapter, and the ones to come afterward.

Do you remember in our first chapter we told the story of the empathic girl who helped a suicidal man? Always keep that story in your mind, especially as you read the next section. We need to cover the potential downsides of being an empath, so you know exactly what to expect.

As an empath, you are very emotionally intelligence, and that opens itself up to possible disadvantages too. Feelings are unpredictable and wild on occasion, and much of the time they can't be controlled. What you need to remember is that feelings are only temporary, and are never a permanent state of mind, especially when they are not your own.

The main negative points of being an empath however are:

- **You feel the emotions of others, not only good but mostly bad** - As humans, we tend to feel negative more than we feel positive. As a result, your empathic nature means that you're going to feel more negative emotions than you deserve to feel. You have your own negative feelings (we all have them on occasion) as well as everyone else's too.

- **An increased chance of developing anxiety and depression** - Feeling all of this negativity can be stressful and extremely overwhelming. It's no surprise that someone with an empathic nature has a higher chance of becoming depressed or anxious as a result of everything that is going on. This is far more likely when that person doesn't know how to center themselves and control their gift. By learning these tools, you'll drastically reduce the chances of this happening to you, and even eradicate it completely.

- **You are so sensitive, even the news is stressful** - If you watch the news and become extremely emotionally distressed at what you're seeing, you'll probably start to avoid reading it or watching it. That's not surprising. The problem is, you're cutting yourself off from the world by doing that. Again, coping mechanisms will help you learn to balance.

- **People seek to take advantage of kind-hearted people** - You're a kind and open-hearted kind of person and that means that you are unfortunately open to those who like to take advantage of this. We mentioned narcissists and energy vampires, and it's vital that you start to learn how to spot these people and get away from them before they have the chance to feed on your endless emotional pool.

- **Every day is a whirlpool of emotions** - You can feel a huge number of emotions within the spectrum within 24 hours. You can start the day feeling happy and content, and by the end of the day you've experienced extreme anger and sadness, gone back to feeling fine, felt ashamed and scared, and then ended the day simply feeling totally exhausted. Being able to soak up the emotions of others is a physically and mentally draining thing but taking time out for yourself and learning how to manage your gift will reduce the tiredness and symptoms you experience.

- **You're likely to become very tired, quite easily** - Again, this is down to feel so many emotions within a short space of time. It's so easy to become mentally drained and you start to feel physically achy and ill as a result. Have regular bouts of being with people and on your own, and recognize when you're starting to feel overwhelmed. By doing that, you can take yourself out of the equation, before the problem becomes too much to bear.

- **You might struggle with romantic relationships** - Not all empaths struggle to form romantic relationships, but many do. The start of a relationship is confusing enough, without having to deal with your emotions and someone else's too! Many empaths also worry about losing themselves within the relationship and as a result, they avoid any type of romantic union. This is a shame because empaths have an endless pool of love to give. We're going to talk about how you can form lasting and fulfilling romantic relationships as an empath in a later chapter.

A person who knows they are an empath but can't cope with it, e.g. they haven't learned how to manage it, or someone who is completely aware of their gift will find everything a struggle. There is a lot of good news coming your way, however - by learning the tricks to manage the gift of empathy, and by knowing your own personal boundaries, you can maximize the potential of being an empath, and minimize the effects.

Now it's time to be positive!

Chapter 3
The Gift of Being an Empath

To a large degree we've focused on the negatives so far, but now that is all about to change. It's time to be positive about your gift and to realize the wonderful good you can do with it. Once you realize how positive it can be, you'll be inspired to take the steps towards learning how to manage its possible ill effects and therefore be better placed to help others.

In order to arrive at that place of acceptance and positivity for the future, you need to see your empathy as a gift. It's not something you're burdened with, and it's not something you've been stuck with and can't get rid of, it's something that you should cherish and enjoy. Let's explore why being an empath is actually a true gift.

7 Reasons Why Being an Empath is a Gift

- **Being an empath will help you focus on positivity** - As you learn to manage your gift, you'll be able to easily recognize negativity. The natural result is that you focus more on positivity and that in itself breeds a greater sense of confidence and happiness.
- **You can choose a career path with real meaning** - Being an empath is something you should certainly count as

resume-worthy! In a short while we're going to talk about some potential career paths you can look into, which will really help with reaching your potential, but for now, you should understand that being an empath means you can do a job which will really mean something and help others as a result.

- **You naturally help others avoid conflict** - An empath can naturally bring people together because of a real dislike for conflict. It's likely that you can't stand to watch people fighting or arguing and that it makes you equally as upsetting. As a result, you're likely to try and help them sort the problem out, bringing them together. That's a wonderful thing!

- **You will be true to yourself** - Empaths can't stand anything false or forced, and that means that any decision you make will be one which is deeply considered and balanced. This means that your overall decision making will be high quality, avoiding regret in the future.

- **You can experience more positive emotions** - We've talked so much about having to deal with your own negative emotions as well as the negative emotions of other people, but let's turn that on its head - you have your own positive emotions, and those of others too! That means you're getting more joy, and that's never a bad thing.

- **You can help other people** - This is the biggest plus point! By being able to pinpoint the emotions of another person, you can help them in very positive ways. Remember the story of the girl who helped the suicidal man? Need we say more?

- **You will be able to rely on your instincts** - By learning to listen to your instincts and trust them, you'll be able to live your life in a more calm and balanced way. Decision making will also be far easier and more reliable. You're able to spot lies and deceit quite far away, and therefore protect yourself and those close to you.

The Ability to Help Others on a Deeper Level

Without a doubt, the biggest plus point of being an empath is the ability to help other people on a far deeper level than anyone else can. The fact you can feel emotions without someone having to actually tell you 'I'm down', 'I'm sad', I'm scared', 'I'm angry' means that you can tap into their problems and help them. Not everyone likes to vocalize when they're feeling something negative.

For instance, let's give another example, and again, this is a true story.

A young man in his late teenage years had a cousin in High School. She was not her usual self and her parents were voicing concerns about her happiness. The young man hadn't seen his cousin for a few years, but his parents mentioned that his auntie, uncle, and cousin would be coming for dinner that Sunday. The moment the young girl walked through the door, the young man felt a maelstrom of emotions. He knew immediately that she was extremely unhappy, scared, and didn't know what to do. Of course, he had no idea why she felt this way, but he knew that whatever she was going through, she needed help.

When their parents had gone into the garden, the young man simply said 'hey, I know something's wrong, I can tell you're really down and scared about something. Are you going to tell me what it is?' It turned out that the young girl was being bullied by two other girls in her class. She had been skipping school several days a week to try and avoid them and she was scared her parents were going to find out too.

If the young man hadn't picked up on it, anything could have happened. People who go through negative times without help and support can be driven towards actions which are extremely devastating for them, and for those around them. The fact that this young man managed to pick up on what was wrong and encourage her to talk, with his empathic and trusting nature, meant that the girl finally found the strength to tell her parents what was going on, and the issue was slowly resolved from there. That is the real gravity of how amazing the gift of empathy can be. You are able to help people on levels which nobody else can. You have this knack of naturally helping people to open up to you; they might not have the first clue why they suddenly feel so calm and relaxed around you, and why they trust you enough to spill their feelings, but they do, and it's a wonderful thing. There is a reason why people say that empaths are 'Earth Angels'. You do good deeds simply by being aware of what other people are going through, and whilst it might come at a cost to you, there are ways to minimize those effects, and keep you doing these amazing things for other people.

Potential Career Paths to Unleash Your Empathic Potential

There are certain natural career paths which are suited to empaths. By choosing a path which encompasses your empathic nature, you can help other people ten times more, but you can also help yourself, by being more in tune with your gift. By doing this, you are far less likely to be negatively affected or overwhelmed by it.

A few career ideas to unleash your true empathic potential are:

* Doctor or nurse

* Counselor

* Therapist

* Teacher

* Psychologist

* Writer

* Artist

* Musician

* Life coach

* Vet

* Social worker

Of course, you could also volunteer in your spare time if you find that you can't change your career path, or you simply don't want to because you enjoy the job you have currently. Volunteering will allow you to make a difference and also regain some balance of your own emotions. Creative routes such as music, writing, and art are a fantastic way for you to pour out the things which are within you emotionally, and bring you greater balance overall.

If you do choose to do any of the jobs we've suggested, you will certainly need to make sure that you can handle and control your empathic nature well, otherwise, you run the risk of being overwhelmed on a daily basis. Of course, you're going to read the rest of this book and learn those techniques however, so that shouldn't be an issue!

Chapter 4
What Are Spiritual Healing Tools?

From this point onwards we're going to give you practical and helpful advice. This advice will allow you to manage your gift and avoid the negative downsides which are associated with being an empath. Spiritual healing tools may be of great help to you and these are things you should learn a little more about.

Of course, these tools may not be for you and you may not be able to connect with them on any level - that's fine; spirituality is a personal thing and what works for one person may not work for another. What you should do however is open your mind to at least trying them out, and only then you really can make a firm decision on whether these tools are helpful to you or not.

This chapter is going to outline a few of those tools before touching on techniques to help you separate your own emotions from those of other people. Meditation is also something you might like to try, and whilst this is something many people find difficult at first, it certainly can be learned, with a little perseverance.

Spiritual Healing Tools to Help You as an Empath

Learning how to protect yourself from negative energies is vital if you want to live a balanced and happy life as an empath. There are many ways you can achieve that protection; some methods are self-help, e.g. taking time out for yourself and using the power of nature, but some are a little more towards the spiritual side.

If you don't consider yourself a particularly spiritual person, it's certainly still worth giving these tools a try. You will, however, need to open your mind and attempt to believe that they will work. A lot of the power of these types of tools is in your belief system. The power of the mind is a wonderful thing.

We'll cover three of the most common and the easiest, to begin with. Many empaths also move more towards the spiritual side of chakras and spirit guides to help block out negative energies, but this is something you can explore yourself if you feel the need to do so. For now, let's stick with the more 'mainstream' methods to try first of all.

Crystals and Stones
There are many different crystals and stones, and all have particular qualities. For instance, if you want to be more confident in yourself and attract love, you should wear rose quartz, and if you want to attract abundance, you should go for green colored stones, such as citrine or green jade. Black colored stones such as black tourmaline, obsidian and onyx are known to be protective stones and have a certain amount of grounding

power, which is vital for an empath who wants to protect themselves from negative energies.

All you need to do is carry the stone with you and hold it in your hand when you're starting to feel a little overwhelmed. You could even try meditating with the stone if you want a little extra power, and we'll talk about meditation in a short while. Many empaths choose to wear protective stones and crystals as pieces of jewelry, e.g. a necklace, as a constant source of protection.

Visualizing Your Own Personal Shield
A very common and useful method of protection is visualization, and this comes in the form of imagining an energy shield around you, which stops any negativity from entering into your space. This is particularly useful if you're out in public, e.g. if you're sat at a bus stop and someone stands next to you who is particularly emotional. By imagining this shield around you, wrapped tight like a protective barrier, which nothing can penetrate, you are mentally pushing away emotions which may otherwise have the power to overwhelm you.

Imagining a personal shield takes practice, but the more you do it, the easier it will be to call upon it in times of need. Practice at home first of all and it might also be useful to image your shield as a color; this makes it easier to see in your mind's eye. Many people opt for white light.

Smudging
Smudging is a form of spiritual tool, which basically sweeps negative energies away from your home. This makes your home a space of sanctuary and somewhere you can escape to, in order

to regroup and recharge yourself at the end of a long day. Smudging itself involves burning herbs and many people find that either too difficult or too overpowering to their senses - remember that empaths often have a very strong and sensitive sense of smell. A good alternative, with the same results, is to burn incense instead.

You might think using another strong-smelling item is against the sentence we've just written, but incense has known calming effects. However, you do need to make sure that you go for high-quality incense and not the cheap versions you will find in your local supermarket!
By burning incense and allowing it to rid your home of negative energies, you're creating a more balanced and positive space.

In order to use this form of smudging you simply need an incense holder, a stick of incense and a candle. You then simply light the stick from the candle flame, remembering to blow out the candle as soon as the incense has lit, carefully place the stick into the holder, so it doesn't fall over, and that's it! Simply let the incense burn until it has finished, and your home should be free of negativity.

These few spiritual healing tools are certainly ideal for beginners and don't require a huge amount of equipment in order to give them a try. Of course, one size doesn't fit all, so be sure to try a few before settling on the method which works for you. It could also be that spiritual healing tools just aren't your thing, and in that case, it's going to be more about allowing yourself time away from others, setting boundaries, and self-care. These are all things we will talk about in a later chapter.

How to Separate Your Emotions from Those of Others

One of the biggest problems for an empath is learning how to separate their emotions, from those of others around them. This can be extremely difficult, especially for someone who is yet to really get a handle on their emotions and the way they feel as an empath. Understanding how to separate your emotions from those around you is the first step to really being able to protect yourself as an empath. By knowing when you're experiencing the transfer of emotions from someone else, you can extract yourself from the situation far more easily, before you become overwhelmed.

The question is, however, how can you be sure whether it is someone else's emotions you're feeling, and not your own? Becoming mindful of the way you are feeling every single day is a good starting point, and in that case, a journal is a great idea.

Every day before you go to work write a few words down which sum up the way you're feeling. If you've woken up feeling tired and a little moody, write it down if you've woken up feeling fine, with nothing really of note to report, write that down too. At lunchtime, do the same thing, and again when you finish work. This exercise will help you become more at one with what your emotional state is, and you can then pinpoint when someone else's emotions are coming towards you much easier. You will obviously need to repeat this for a short while so that it becomes second nature to you, but the more you do it, the more effective it will be.

Being mindful of your own emotional state is the single best way to be able to separate your feelings from those of others, but you can also be mindful of the way your feelings change when you are around other people. For instance, you might suddenly start to feel differently, and the fact that the change happened rapidly will be informed enough to tell you that these emotions aren't yours. In that case, you can leave the situation far easier than otherwise. Staying in that situation for too long, falsely thinking that the emotions are actually yours, is a fast-track towards empathic burnout, something we're going to talk about in more detail later on.

The Art of Meditation

One of the best ways for an empath to really ground and center themselves is by learning the art of meditation.

The problem with meditation is that many people have a false idea of what it is, and as a result, they avoid trying it for themselves. Meditation doesn't have to be difficult, and it doesn't have to involve chanting or any type of special moves. Meditation can be as simple as being quiet and turning your thoughts inwards, or simply being mindful of the things which are around you. What every type of meditation requires, however, is the ability to be able to quieten the mind.

We live in very stressful and busy times, and we are rarely ever disconnected and at peace from the things which are circling around us. For instance, we always have our phones with us, we're always on social media, there is always music in the background, perhaps the TV on, the radio when we're driving, people talking wherever we go. This constant chatter and white noise can be distracting, and when you're attempting to meditate, you need to be able to cut out this out and focus on your breath. By doing this, you can explore answers to problems, but you can also simply give yourself time to 'be', and to stay in your original emotional state, without being affected by the feelings of anyone else around you.

So, how to begin meditating?

There are countless different types of meditation, but for an empath, there are two main methods to try as a starting point. Let's explore these now.

Method 1 - Self-Awareness
This particular meditation exercise allows you to turn off your reactions to the outside world and to turn everything internal. This means that you focus only on yourself and your own feelings. The more you practice this type of meditation, the easier it will become, so don't worry if the first few times you can't quite manage to turn off the noise, or actually get yourself into a quiet state.

1. Make yourself comfortable, either sitting in a comfortable chair or lying down in bed. If you're cold, grab a blanket, etc.

You need to be comfortable temperature-wise and in terms of how light or dark it is, in order to avoid your mind becoming distracted.

2. Close your eyes and focus on your breathing. Breathe in through your nose for a count of five, in a slow and even manner. Pause for a count of three, and then exhale through your mouth in the same slow and even manner, for another count of five. Continue this throughout the exercise. This type of breathing is very useful for many different situations, e.g. if you're feeling anxious, panicked, or you need to turn attention inwards in general.

3. Once you feel relaxed, turn your attention towards your toes. Scan for any aches or discomfort in the area. It might help to tense the part of your body you're focusing on, hold it for a few seconds and then release.

4. Once you've finished scanning your toes, move to your feet and repeat the process. Slowly make your way up your entire body. By the time you reach the top of your head, you should be completely calm and focused, without any outside interferences.

Once you get yourself into this deeply relaxed state, do not put pressure on yourself to feel or do anything. Simply focus on your body and the way it feels when you think about a certain part of your body, or when you tense up and relax. Relaxation is so vital for empaths, and this is something you could try and do on a regular basis, to really grab the benefits. This particular exercise also helps to make you far more self-aware, and that will be a great source of protection against negative energies. It will also help you become more aware of the emotions that are yours, versus those from other people.

When you're ready to come out of your meditative state, simply set out your intention and allow yourself to come back 'to' in a slow and even manner. Don't suddenly sit up as this could be a rather abrupt shock to the system! Lay still for a few minutes and slowly sit up, bringing your attention and awareness back to the room calmly.

Method 2 - Mindfulness
Mindfulness meditation is one of the easiest starting points for anyone to try because you don't necessarily need to do anything other than be aware of what is around you. It is far better to practice this type of meditation outside, e.g. within any type of nature, as it will hold more power for you and therefore have greater benefits. You can do this type of meditation whilst you're walking to work.

1. Repeat the breathing exercise from the self-awareness meditation, e.g. breathing in through your nose, pausing, and exhaling through your mouth. You can do this without closing your eyes, you simply need to focus your attention on your breath entirely.

2. Look around you and notice the small details. For instance, notice the leaves on the trees you're walking past and how green they are, notice the feel of the wind against your skin, the noise it makes as it gently whistles past. The more aware you are of your actual surroundings, you're taking your

attention away from your emotions, and therefore ground yourself whilst you're outside.

As you can see, mindfulness meditation is by far the easiest method, but it takes focus and practice even still.

If you want to continue your meditation journey there are many other types of meditation you can try, including guided meditation. This may be useful if you're really struggling to focus yourself and you need a more formal and rigid exercise. This type of meditation is usually done in a class, which may not be ideal for an empath, and in that case, why not download a podcast and try it at home? You simply listen to the words and follow the instructions.

Chapter 5
How to Fight Negative Energy

Negative energy really is the enemy of an empath. The positive energy which will come your way, from other people, isn't an issue - nobody has a problem with feeling more joy on a daily basis! Negative energies are far more prevalent, mainly because these types of energies are stronger, and are therefore easier to transfer.

For example, most people would agree that anger is a stronger emotion than joy. When you're angry you feel it in every fiber of your being. It causes your body to act in a certain way, and it makes you feel physically uptight and full of rage. This is a very drastic and strong emotion, and whilst joy is also powerful, it doesn't exhibit the same level. This is why empaths are far more likely to feel negative emotions than positive ones, and it's also a fact that stress, depression, and anxiety are on the rise amongst the general population. The more people feeling these emotional negativities, the more chance of it actually being transferred to an innocent bystander, e.g. an empath.

For that reason, being able to fight negative energies, with a few prevention methods, is vital.

How Negative Energy Directly Impacts on an Empath

We've just mentioned that negative emotions are more prevalent generally than positive ones, and that means that during the course of a day, you're sure to feel something negative if you're out and about in a busy space. These negative emotions can quickly turn your day from good to bad, by the very fact that you absorb them like a sponge.

This can be damaging in several ways, but it can often reach the point where an empath is waiting for negative to come their way, they're almost second guessing it. This type of anticipation doesn't lead to long-term happiness and can actually increase your risk of anxiety and depression. If you're always on the lookout for negativity, how can you be happy? It makes it ten times worse than that negativity isn't even yours!

Negativity is exhausting, and it can also lead an empath to feel very tired towards the end of the day. Knowing when to extract yourself from a situation is vital, but sometimes you can't do it, e.g. at work. In this case, the spiritual healing tools we mentioned earlier, such as visualizing a protective shield around you, may help.

To sum up how negative energy directly impacts on an empath:

• Increases your chances of stress, anxiety, and depression

- Can lead you towards always anticipating negativity, which further increases your chances of depression

- Can exhaust you and leave you feeling drained and tired at the end of the day

- May cause you to avoid social situations, to try and also avoid the negative energies that may come your way

The Possible Outcomes of Not Being Grounded

Being grounded is about practicing self-awareness and being 'at one' with yourself. Meditation will help you do this, as will writing your emotions down in a journal on a daily basis. By being grounded, you're helping yourself avoid these negative energies. When you're not grounded, you're basically not in control of your empathy at all. Someone who hasn't yet learned how to manage the gift of being an empath isn't grounded; they don't know how to control it and they don't know what to do in order to avoid the negative sides of it. This lack of grounding can lead them towards losing their identity and not being able to separate their feelings from the feelings of those around them. The problem is that grounding can be hard to learn at first, and for someone who is very sensitive, like an empath, even the smallest thing, and the smallest change in vibration, can cause all manner of issues to come your way. The good news is that grounding isn't as hard as you might think.

A few ways to ground yourself include:

- Any type of physical activity will ground you immediately

- Meditation

- Spending time within yourself, e.g alone, in nature, and exploring your emotions/self-reflection

- Visualization - Imagine your feet have roots attached to the bottom, and they go down into the Earth, connecting you with the ground

- Using crystals - We mentioned black crystals for grounding earlier

By not being grounded, you're prone to being knocked off course by the slightest gust of wind!

Methods to Fight Negative Energy

Now it's time for some practical advice!

There are certain things which empaths do, and these methods are ideal for fighting negative emotions and causing less impact on daily life. Try a few of these and see which work for your particular situation. As before, not everything we talk about is going to work for you, because every single person is different, and your uniqueness means that one size doesn't fit all! There are bound to be a few which will work for you, however, and in that case, simply focus on those.

These are some of the most commonly used methods for fighting negative energy, whilst also grounding you in the process.

3. Limit the amount of time you spend in large groups

4. Ensure that when you have downtime, you spend it doing things you enjoy, e.g. reading, going out for a walk in nature, swimming, etc

5. Ensure you get enough sleep - an empath who is lacking in sleep will find it much harder to be able to fight off negative energies

6. Use a visualized energy shield - imagine a shield of light all around you, with no gap for any negative energy to permeate through

7. Make sure you get plenty of physical exercises - this grounds you and also helps you become stronger physically and emotionally

8. Try meditation in order to become more self-aware

9. Set boundaries with those around you who you know are going to pass their emotions over unwittingly. This could mean limiting the amount of time you spend with them or asking them not to unload their feelings onto you via a conversation

10. Learn to say 'no' - empaths find it very hard to say 'no' to someone, e.g. if a person wants to talk about a problem, etc. If you are in the midst of an energy vampire, spending more time with them is simply going to exhaust you even more. It's perfectly fine to walk away from that person and make your excuses. You don't have to explain yourself! Practice self-care.

11. Become more aware of how you become drained, e.g. is it a situation, a person, etc. By knowing your personal drains, you can limit your time there or avoid them altogether.

12. Use positive affirmations on a daily basis to keep your mindset away from the negative

13. Create an effective method for releasing pent up emotion, e.g. going into a field and shouting at the top of your lungs, or perhaps trying kick-boxing, or another type of sporting activity. This will keep you away from unhealthy coping mechanisms. Yoga is also a very useful method of releasing pent up emotion in a positive way.

14. Make sure you have plenty of 'you' time. We mentioned spending your downtime doing things you love, but make sure that you actually schedule in this time in the first place!

As you can see, there is nothing particularly tricky about any of those methods, but they all work really well in terms of grounding you as an empath, and also protecting and fighting against negative energies. The good news is that the more you fight the negative, the more positive you will become, and the more positive emotions you will feel. Remember, being an empath isn't a bad thing, provided you can get a handle on the negatives and control them.

Chapter 6
The Importance of Space and Time

There are two very important things for an empath to have on a regular basis - space for themselves, and time for themselves. As an empath yourself, you'll probably know that spending time alone is one of the greatest things in life because that is a time you can truly be comfortable and avoid any possible vibrations from other people.

Remember, it's impossible to stop vibrations and negative energies coming your way, you can only manage and control them. For a new empath, e.g. someone who has only really just learned what they are and what is happening, this entire process can be extremely tiring. In this case, time alone and space to simply 'be' is vital.

Most empaths are introverted, this is something we've already explored. In general, introverted people have no problem with spending time alone, in fact, they like it! Whilst extroverts prefer to be around people, in social situations, introverts really don't care about the whole social thing. Of course, that doesn't mean that they want to avoid people and don't want to build up relationships and friendships, of course, they do, but they also enjoy time on their own. This is actually a major positive because time alone can be used for self-reflection, something else which an empath needs.

The bottom line is this - as an empath, you're going to be extremely tired and burnt out if you don't make time for yourself. You might want to go around helping everyone, but it's simply not possible without a price being paid - your health and wellbeing. Even those in caring jobs, e.g. nurses and counselors, need a time out from their job; you can't help others if you're not in the greatest space yourself.

Even if you're not really interested in going around doing good deeds, failing to make time and space for yourself is a fast track towards anxiety and depression. You need this time, and you need to be able to connect with yourself. If you don't do this, you'll lose sight of your own emotions and you won't be able to ascertain which feelings are yours, and which belong to someone else.

Of course, the emotions which are transferred to you as an empath from someone else don't stay with you per se. Once that person has left you alone, you'll probably find the feelings dissipate somewhat, but the lingering effect might remain. If that person was feeling extremely angry about something and you started to exhibit signs of anger, you'll probably feel less angry once they've gone, but it might bring up the memory of something which happened a few days, which actually made you feel angry personally. This then rehashes old wounds and creates a 'living in the past' scenario. Nothing good ever came from living in the past.

Limiting Time Spent with Others

It's not just important to make time for yourself, but it's also important to limit your time around people who drag you down emotionally. Remember, this person isn't doing it on purpose; they have no idea that they are transferring their emotions to you, because they're simply feeling them and trying to deal with them - your empathic nature is soaking it up, they're not doing it intentionally! It can be very easy to become annoyed or angry with people who are unknowingly transferring a feeling in your direction, and that's why it's important to set boundaries and limit your time.

For example, if you're going to a social gathering, perhaps a birthday party and you really can't get out of it, then make sure you have a way out if you need it. Many empaths choose to take their own cars to such gatherings so they can leave when they want without much hassle. You could also set yourself a time you are going to leave, and make your excuses, e.g. 'I've got an early start in the morning, but I had a lovely time, I hope you enjoyed your birthday'. That is polite and you still showed up, without having to deal with serious negative energy coming your way.

In addition, if you start to feel overwhelmed have some coping mechanisms in place, e.g. using your visualized energy shield, or simply set yourself a boundary in terms of how you feel when you want to leave. You will know when you've had enough, but make sure that your personal boundary is before that, e.g. before you reach the point of being overwhelmed.

You also need to be sure that you are spending time with the right people. As an empath, you want to help others and you want to be a shoulder to cry on, but you also need to put yourself first on occasion. Being there for everyone else is not going to be any good for you if you're absolutely exhausted every single night before bed, and you spend the first hour tossing and turning, going over everything in your head. Make sure that you are spending time around people who make you feel uplifted and positive, and limit your time, or even avoid, those who make you feel anything different.

Most empaths have a hard time walking away from toxic relationships and friendships because they are good people and don't want to believe that someone else might not be. The problem is, it's important to realize that not everyone has the same heart as you, otherwise you're going to go through life becoming hurt time and time again. Monitor how you feel when you spend time with certain people in your life and make a decision based on that information.

The Best Ways to Spend Your Down Time

It's not just about limiting time around people, it's about spending your downtime in the most productive of ways - time spent nourishing your soul!

We've mentioned nature time and time again, and if you can do anything which has a connection to Mother Nature, you'll feel more grounded and far more emotionally balanced as a result.

Swimming is great because it is physical exercise, which we all need, it helps to ground you, and it also has that natural connection to water. If you don't want to get your hair wet, simply going out for a walk with the dog, or on your own is a great way to spend time your time. Equally, having a hot bath and reading a book, doing some meditation, cooking a meal you love, etc.

The best ways to spend your downtime are always about looking after number one - You!

Empaths and Romantic Relationships

One area which many empaths struggle with is the realm of romance. We mentioned earlier that many empaths actually avoid relationships because they're worried about losing their own identity or drowning in the maelstrom of emotions that a relationship causes. The thing is, empaths are wonderful people and not having someone to spend time with is really a huge shame. Of course, if you truly don't want a relationship at this time in your life, or ever, that's fine; what isn't fine is craving that connection but avoiding it out of fear.

It's entirely possible for an empath to have a very fulfilling and loving relationship, and it's simply about setting boundaries and having an understanding partner. For starters, an empath is not going to have a great relationship with someone who doesn't believe in empaths and doesn't understand them. In order for this union to work, the partner has to know what empathy is, how it affects their partner, and how it makes them feel on a daily basis. Only when someone really understands what it means to be an empath can they really know that person and what makes them tick.

For instance, an empath likes to spend time alone. If they're in a relationship with someone who doesn't understand why they need personal space on occasion, it's just not going to work. The empath is going to feel overwhelmed and burnt out, and it's going to lead towards stress and anxiety. On the other hand, if the partner understands why they need to be alone sometimes and why it's so important, then the empathic partner is going to feel supported and free to have the time they need.

Of course, we also know that empaths are very sensitive, very emotional and highly intuitive. This can lead to a range of different challenges in relationships, so the understanding partner side of things is really just one part of the puzzle. In addition, an empath needs to be able to have clear boundaries in place, which allows them to retreat if they feel overwhelmed.

For example, it may be very easy for an empath to become paranoid about a partner if they get a sense that something isn't quite right. They may pick up on a feeling of them not being the happiest, and because they are so emotionally involved with them on other levels, they may start to think that it's something they've done, or that they're not happy in the relationship. The reality may be quite different, but the seed may have been sewn enough for the empath to want to retreat too quickly.

Boundaries are vital for a healthy relationship in general, but in a relationship with one partner who is an empath, this is even more vital. The other part of the deal is communication. Whilst communication is important in any relationship, in this case, it is certainly even more so.

Chapter 7
How to Deal with Empathic Burnout

One of the most challenging parts of being an empath, especially at the start when you haven't quite got a handle on how to manage it all, is empathic burnout.

Now, you don't necessarily have to be an empath to experience empathic burnout. A person who is quite sensitive to the feelings of others can also easily become burnout if they allow themselves to stay around a situation which sucks the very life out of them. A good example of this is a friend who is going through a tough time. Of course, you want to help them, but they have latched onto you because they know you will listen to them. You offer a shoulder to cry on, but they don't seem to want to let go of your shoulder any time soon! This leads you to feel tired of saying the same things over and over again, without any change, and it also makes you feel guilty and worried about why you feel that way.

There is no reason to feel bad when you become frustrated with other people. It's completely normal! Nobody needs to or wants to, listen to the same thing on repeat, especially when you're giving advice and they don't seem to want to hear it. In addition, they start calling you when you're at home, trying to spend time with your own loved ones.

This situation is one of the most common which leads to empathic burnout, and it can also lead to someone feeling unsure of which way to turn. The very nature of an empath and those who are quite sensitive is that they want to help people, but drawing the line can be difficult.

Never feel guilty for walking away from a situation which makes you feel overwhelmed or uncomfortable, and never feel guilty for needing time for yourself. These are necessary self-care methods which are required for overall health and wellbeing. If you continue listening to your friend without setting boundaries, you're going to be exhausted, probably manifesting physical symptoms of illness and your friend will be over their problem and happily skipping through their day!

The symptoms of empathic burnout include:

- Feeling extremely tired, borderline exhausted

- Not being able to escape from the situation which is causing the burnout

- Feelings from the past being brought to the surface, e.g. if your friend is talking about the fact that their partner cheated on them, this may lead you to remember a similar situation in your past, and you'll, therefore, start to relive those negative feelings for yourself

- Not being able to get away from the emotions of the other person

- A sense of not being grounded or self-aware

- Possible physical symptoms include headaches, lethargy, fatigue, lack of energy and focus

- Wanting to retreat from the outside world

As you can see, empathic burnout symptoms are very similar to general burnout, and they're no less serious! When you're in the midst of a situation which is causing you to feel overwhelmed and burnt out, your body and mind are under extreme stress. Stress is very dangerous for the mind and body, especially when the situation is prolonged or severe.

Easy Steps to Deal with Empathic Burnout

So, how can you deal with empathic burnout and avoid it from happening in the first place? Yet again it's about boundaries, but it's also about learning to say 'no'.

In the example we gave, it's very hard for someone who is an empath to turn away from a person they care about because they can feel how down and sad they are. The problem is, if you don't find the strength to walk away for at least a short while, you're going to end up feeling extremely low yourself. Empaths don't often put themselves first, but you need to learn how to start.

Let's cover how you would deal with the above situation, and from there you can adapt it to suit the types of situations you might encounter in the future.

- Start to set boundaries with your friend, and only be available at certain times - Being available 24/7 isn't going to do your health any good, and because your friend is so desperate for someone to talk to, it's likely that they will continue to talk to you whenever they feel the need. You can be there for them, but only when it really does suit you. So, don't answer your phone when you're at home with your own partner or family, or when you simply want to spend time alone. Put it onto silent so you don't hear it and then you won't be tempted to just answer and spend five minutes with them. By doing this, you're helping them too, because, in order for them to move on from the problem, they need to deal with things and move on - you cannot be their emotional crutch forever.

- Give yourself a whole weekend to yourself - Yes, an entire weekend! The world is not going to stop turning because you're not there for everyone who demands your time and attention, and instead it's vital that you turn everything inwards and spend time doing the things you love. Nourish your soul; read books, watch films, have a hot bath, pamper yourself, play some sports, watch the TV programs you enjoy and basically be as selfish as you like - you have permission! When the weekend is over, by all means, turn your phone back on and speak to your friend again, but you need the time to be able to recharge your own batteries and avoid burnout from becoming a huge problem.

- Whenever you feel the stirrings of burnout happening, revert back to the first step and do what you need to do, for as long as you need to do it. By looking after number one, you're not being selfish in a bad way, you're simply looking after your health and wellbeing, and that is more important than anything else.

Regularly using the self-help tricks we've talked about throughout the book will also help you avoid empathic burnout, but there are probably going to be odd times when it sneaks through, e.g. when a very strong emotional situation crops up. When you notice this happening, it's important to extract yourself from the situation as quickly as you can. Strong emotions can knock an empath off their feet.

No, You're Not Being 'Too Sensitive'

The most important thing to remember about being an empath or even simply being highly sensitive to the emotions of others is that there is nothing wrong with you. Never let anyone tells you that empathy is a negative trait or something which doesn't exist in real life o you feel it every single day; it's real, and it's part of who you are.

You are not being 'too sensitive', and your empathy isn't something you should hide or be ashamed of. The thing is, if you take away your empathy, you also take away other traits that make up who you are too, such as your creativity, your intuition, your attention to detail, your caring nature, your ability to know what to say at the right time, and your kindness too. Empaths may have a hard time on occasion, but the benefits far outweigh the negatives, provided you can find a way to balance everything and set boundaries to avoid burnout from occurring.

Those who accuse you of being 'too sensitive' simply don't understand what empathy is; it's quite likely that these types of people have no empathy, and that in itself is a problem. An empath doesn't find it easy to be around someone who lacks empathy, a little like a narcissist in many ways. This type of person cannot understand why emotions and feelings are so important, and they belittle them to mean nothing. What they don't understand is that emotions are part of being human, they are chemical reactions and things which are 100% real. If you went through life not feeling anything, how boring would that be?

You should never allow yourself to feel shame or embarrassment when it comes to your empathic gift, and those who say that you're simply too sensitive or weak, really have no clue how strong you are. The ability to handle several strong emotions in one day takes strength and guts. Always remember that!

If you take anything away from this book, make it this last section, and never allow yourself to feel less than your best because of your empathic ability.

Find Your Own Path

We're nearing the end of our book now, and that means that you know almost everything there is to know about empathy, and how to deal with being an empath. What we need to point out before we move onto our FAQ section is that one size doesn't fit all.

We've touched upon this already, but it's really worth reiterating - just because one person deals with empathy by being able to say 'no' to people they don't want to be around, it doesn't mean you're going to find it so easy. Just because we've mentioned that smudging works for some people, it doesn't mean that it's going to work for you. It really comes down to the things which fit your personality and your beliefs.

Mediation is something which is hugely beneficial for empaths, but it isn't an easy thing to learn. For that reason, many empaths give up before they reap the benefits. If you find that medication really isn't coming easily to you and you really don't see how it is ever going to help you, then perhaps it really isn't the right path for you. In that case, maybe simple mindfulness or spending time alone is a better option.

As you move through your life as an empath, you really will find your own individual path. This path will allow you to traverse the challenges that life will throw your way, and you'll learn methods which help you to deal with hurdles and potholes too. The things we've talked about in this book are meant to be for guidance, and the options you choose to pursue are your personal choice. Never feel that you're failing because you can't get a particular technique to work at the beginning, you're unique and that means your approach has to be equally so.

Chapter 8
Frequently Asked Questions

If you need to quickly refer back to something in the book, you might not have time to read through in its entirety, in that case, our frequently asked questions (FAQ) section is going to be a fantastic time saver for you!

Some of these FAQs might seem simple, some might seem a little more complicated, but for overall completeness and understanding, let's give a quick reference guide to the wonderful world of being an empath.

Aren't empathy and empath the same thing?
They sound like they are, but they're actually distinctly different. Empathy is the ability to understand and connect with the feelings of other people, and to really see things from their point of view. Being an empath means you actually feel those emotions as though they are your own, simply by being close to or spending a little time with someone. You don't even have to know the person that well, or at all.

Can't I just turn off the ability to soak up these emotions?
Being an empath can be hard, but there is no way to turn it all off. You shouldn't want to turn it off, being an empath is a true gift, you just need to learn how to manage it and control it. So

no, there is no 'cure' for being an empath, nor should there be - there is nothing wrong with you!

Is there anything I can take to drown it all out?

Again, no. Being an empath isn't a medical issue or something which needs to be stopped, it simply needs to be managed in order to make life a little easier.

I can't differentiate between my own emotions and those of other people, is this normal?

This is a very common issue for empaths who haven't yet learned how to manage or control their gift. And it is a gift. By becoming more self-aware you will find it easier to differentiate between emotions which are your own, and those from other people. You will also notice that emotions that do not belong to you disappear very quickly, e.g. when the person has gone from your space, or when you take yourself away from that person. All emotions are transient and are not permanent.

I can't meditate, what do I do?

You don't have to! Meditation is certainly a very useful coping mechanism for empaths who want to avoid burnout, but it's not the only way. Many people struggle to learn how to meditate, but it's not something that is impossible, it just takes perseverance and time. The ability to turn off the outside noise and focus on yourself isn't easy, especially in the busy world we live in, but practice will make perfect in this case.

Do empaths have psychic abilities?

No. There is a very real difference between empathy and those who have paranormal psychic abilities. Empathy is a gift, that's a truth, but it's not a way of looking into the future or having visions, it's simply about being able to understand and feel what someone else is feeling. You have no idea what they are going through, but you know how they feel. Only by talking to them can you ascertain the reason for their emotions.

Do they have flashes into what the person is experiencing?
No. As we've just mentioned, whilst an empath does fall under the spiritual umbrella, it isn't a psychic ability. There are no flashbacks or visions into what is causing a person to feel the way they are feeling.

What are the main downsides of being an empath?
Negative emotions and energies can be very difficult to deal with, especially when they are not your own. It is also very tiring spiritually, emotionally, and physically to experience so many emotions within the space of one day. Empaths are also very sensitive and can be hurt easily - certain types of people can easily take advantages of that, such as narcissists and energy vampires.

What are the benefits of being an empath?
It's not all bad! Empaths feel the positive emotions of others as well as the negative, so that means double the dose of joy! Empaths are also very well placed to help others and that is never a bad thing.

Can I use my empathic ability for good?
Yes, you can, and it's definitely encouraged. There are many specific professions which suit an empath really well, such as a nurse, doctor, teacher, counselor, life guidance coach, youth

coach, volunteer, as well as any creative type of career which may inspire others, e.g, writer, artist, or musician, to name a few. You also have the knack of being able to help those in need far easier than many other people can.

Is it possible for an empath to have a normal relationship?
Yes, but it takes three things - an understanding partner, good communication, and boundaries. If these things fall into place then it is entirely possible for an empath to have a normal relationship, and it is likely to be a very loving and close one, thanks to the ability to really feel.

Of course, there are many other questions you might have about empathy in general, but the hope is that you will find the answers throughout this book. These are the main takeaway points to remember.

Conclusion

And there we have it! You now know all you need to know about the deeply emotional world of being an empath. Whether you think you actually are an empath or you simply have a high sensitivity level to the feelings of others, the information and coping techniques we've covered in this book will help you traverse the challenges that may come your way.

It's vital that you realize empathy is a gift and not something to be scared or, or something to try and ignore. It is a part of who you are, and by embracing it, and learning how to manage and control its inevitable downsides, you can really harness its power and use it for the greater good. It's not all about helping other people either, because empathy will also allow you to feel joy on a greater level than before. You might focus on the negatives, but life isn't all about darkness; there is a lot of joy to be found too, and your empathic ability will show you small random acts of kindness in the least likely of places.

The main coping techniques that you need to try and adopt, or at least try, are:

- Setting boundaries

- Having plentiful 'me' time

- Learning how to ground yourself

- Meditation techniques and mindfulness

- Letting nature help you

- Looking after yourself generally, getting enough sleep, exercising regularly, eating properly, etc.

- Understanding that saying 'no' isn't a bad thing

- Learning to appreciate those who lift you up and make you feel positive

- Using visualization, e.g. a protective shield

There are many other methods which head into the realms of spirituality, and it's entirely up to you whether you want to use those or stick to the more mainstream methods. Everyone has their own ways of coping, and that means finding a path which suits you and your needs.

The main takeaway point to remember is that you should never be ashamed or upset about your gift as an empath. More and more people are becoming aware of the fact that they have these kinds of abilities, and when you really start to understand why you've been so easily hurt in the past, and why everything seems to be magnified emotionally, it will feel like a weight has been lifted off your shoulders - finally you have a name for the way you've been feeling and what you've been experiencing, and you realize there is absolutely nothing wrong with you at all, and plenty of things right with you!

Most empaths are confused about why they are so sensitive and why they are hurt so easily, they can't understand why the news affects them so deeply and why they seem to feel so many emotions within one day. Then, out of nowhere, they read about this thing called 'being an empath' and it's like someone switched on a light. It's likely that this book has done the same thing for you, and with that, you should be feeling uplifted and positive.

The future as an empath is very bright, and there is a lot of good that you can do with your gift. All you need to do is harness its potential and direct it towards the positive, keeping it firmly away from the negative. If you can do that then you will find that life isn't as hard as it was before, and you aren't jumping from emotion to emotion without any control. You have the reins in your hand, you have total control over where you go and what happens to your - emotions do not define you, they enhance you.

Victor Murphy

9 781699 174180